CHRIST'S LAST
COMMAND

CHRIST'S LAST COMMAND

PETER A. STEVESON

JOURNEY FORTH™

A Division of BJU Press

Greenville, South Carolina

Library of Congress Cataloging-in-Publication Data

Steveson, Peter A. (Peter Allan), 1934-
  Christ's last command : resources for success / Peter A.
Steveson.
      p. cm.
  Summary: "This is a book about Christ's last command to share
the gospel and the resources He has given to us to evangelize the
world"—Provided by publisher.
  ISBN-13: 978-1-59166-709-4 (perfect bound pbk. : alk. paper)
  ISBN-10: 1-59166-709-7
  1. Witness bearing (Christianity) 2. Evangelistic work. I. Title.
  BV4520.S6745 2006
  266—dc22

                                                    2006028837

Cover Photo Credits: © 2006 iStockphoto Inc.

All Scripture is quoted from the Authorized King James Version.

Christ's Last Command: Resources for Success

Design by Rita Golden
Composition by Michael Boone

© 2006 BJU Press
Greenville, South Carolina 29614

ISBN-13: 978-1-59166-709-4
ISBN-10: 1-59166-709-7

15 14 13 12 11 10 9 8 7 6 5 4 3 2 1

Dedicated to the memory of Dr. Bob Jones Sr.,
who challenged his "preacher boys"
to load and shoot the gospel gun

TABLE OF CONTENTS

FOREWORD

I APPROACH THE subject of soulwinning with some hesitation. I don't consider myself to be a polished example to teach others. The spiritual gifts the Lord has given me don't include the gift of soulwinning. I'm a plugger, doing my best and occasionally seeing someone come to Christ. I've often described myself as being pigheaded. When I make up my mind to do something, *I will do it*. I may not do it with flair and style, it may not come easily, but it will get done. I made up my mind years ago that I would try to win the lost to the Lord. While I may not be specially gifted in the area, the Lord has given me the privilege of seeing many folks profess faith in Jesus Christ.

Soulwinning is not just for the pastor or the evangelist. It is not just for those who have a spiritual gift in that area. It is for every child of God. So I have tried to be faithful in giving the gospel message to others. Over my forty plus years in the ministry, the Lord has given me the privilege of seeing souls come to Christ everywhere I have served. Some have come in response to sermons I have preached. Some have come from counseling. Many have come as the result of personal work.

This book had its start in a class in personal evangelism that I taught for several years. I taught lay students methods that would help them become better soulwinners. The class forced me to organize my thoughts about witnessing. As I looked back over the years, I realized that the Lord had taken me through experiences that illustrated many different resources He has made available to every Christian. I also drew on personal experiences to develop some comments on the approach to witnessing, the presentation of the gospel, and some practical matters that helped me to become more effective in reaching the lost.

At the first class meeting of each week, I answered questions that came from the students' witnessing activities over the weekend. Many of their questions dealt with common sense matters that were readily handled. But many of the questions reflected basic misunderstandings of their responsibilities as a soulwinner.

Some of the students took the class lightly, fulfilling the requirements but doing the bare minimum just so they could pass the course. Others were more serious, genuinely wanting to become proficient in winning the lost to the Lord. It was always thrilling to hear of a student who had led his first soul to Christ. Unfortunately, more of the students approached the class casually than seriously. I believe that my students probably reflected prevailing attitudes among Christians in the church. This book will help those who are serious. My prayer is that those who are more casual about evangelism will be challenged by something here. You should and you can win the lost to Christ. By God's grace, do it!

THE LORD'S LAST COMMAND

AFTER THE RESURRECTION of Jesus Christ from the tomb in the Garden of Gethsemane, He spent forty days and nights with His closest followers. During that time, He taught them "the things pertaining to the kingdom of God" (Acts 1:3). The Holy Spirit led the biblical authors to give us a short summary of this time. Each of the four Gospel writers as well as Luke's history of the early church in Acts 1 refers to the Lord's teaching after the Resurrection. With almost six weeks of teaching by the resurrected Lord, wouldn't you think that there would be several dozen commands to guide you in your Christian living? Wouldn't you expect to see some commands that would help you by setting up clear Christian standards for you in different areas? Wouldn't you expect to see the doctrines of Christianity taught in a way that no one could confuse or mistake them? It would solve many of the troubling divisions we have in Christianity today if the Lord had taught what the local church should be. Perhaps you might think that He would motivate His followers to faithful service by leaving them with teaching about the glories of heaven and the eternal ages. Instead, you find none of these things. You have exactly one command left by the Lord for His church—the command that His followers should lead the lost to place their faith in Jesus Christ for their salvation. This is the last command from Jesus Christ given to those who have received Him as their Savior and Lord.

Each of the four Gospels and the book of Acts give the command. The New Testament records the command in Matthew 28:19–20; Mark 16:15; Luke 24:46–47; John 20:21–23; and Acts 1:8. These four authors phrase the command differently as they give it, but it is clear that Jesus Christ emphasized the need for evangelism by those who follow Him. Because of this emphasis by the Lord, the members of the early church practiced evangelism. Their practice left a clear example for Christians today; see, for example, Acts 2:38–41; 8:12, 26–37; 10:34–45; 13:38–39; 16:14–15, 30–33.

The Lord's teaching during the forty days with His followers suggests that He did not want to confuse or mislead Christians today. He did not give several commands so that we could pick out the ones we want to obey. He didn't give several choices so that we could decide what area of Christianity we want to specialize in. He didn't deal with so many areas of Christianity that we would be confused. He gave just one command that He expects every Christian to obey: "Ye shall receive power, after that the Holy [Spirit] is come upon you: and ye shall be witnesses unto me" (Acts 1:8a). This witness should start in our Jerusalem, where we live; continue to Samaria and to all Judea, the nearby areas that surround our home; and extend eventually to "the uttermost part of the earth." We should be a witness to Him, telling others that Jesus Christ can save them if they will repent of their sins and accept His death at Calvary as a sacrifice on their behalf.

The command of our Lord is clear, but Christians have a problem carrying out the command. Most Christians do not witness to others regularly about their personal faith in Jesus

Christ. They may bring up the gospel occasionally, but there is very little burden to witness to others as a repeated activity. According to a Barna poll of religious people, only 23 percent of all churchgoers tried to witness during 2003.[1] That number includes many different groups—Pentecostals (who led the way), Baptists, Presbyterians, Roman Catholics. Of those, a much smaller number actually led someone to receive Jesus Christ.

I know from my years in the ministry that many Christian parents do not speak with their children about the need to accept Jesus Christ as their Savior. I think my personal experience is probably typical of many Christian families. My parents were above-average Christians. At various times both taught Sunday school classes. My father was a lay preacher who often led worship services onboard his ship when he was in the navy. Both my mother and father read their Bibles regularly. They took me to church from my earliest years. My father wrote a tract that was published by *The Sword of the Lord*. They held various offices in the church, with my dad even serving as chairman of the deacon board. And yet neither one of them ever sat down with me to give me the gospel. They took me to church every week. They lived godly lives at home and in public. They didn't curse, didn't use cigarettes or alcohol, and were honest and hard working. But they never spoke directly with me about salvation. As a result, I didn't accept the Lord until I was in the eleventh grade in high school, and I didn't begin to live for the Lord until after I was married. I'm fortunate I was in churches that preached the gospel since I didn't receive it in the home.

Later, I had my own problem in trying to win the lost to the Lord. I had begun teaching a Sunday school class of fourth-grade boys. I wasn't prepared to teach. I had never read the Bible through. I hadn't even read the New Testament through. The only thing I knew about the Bible was what I had picked up by half listening to Sunday school lessons and sermons. I had very little experience in teaching and no experience in teaching the Bible. But I had recently rededicated myself to the Lord and so there I was—a willing body with a semigood heart and few qualifications! After several weeks of teaching, one of my boys missed a couple of weeks. I needed to make a call to find out what the problem was. But . . . that particular boy had an unsaved father. And he had the reputation of being hard to talk with. I can remember driving to the house, parking, and walking to the front door. My heart was pounding, my mouth was dry, and I was scared stiff. I rang the doorbell, and, when no one answered, I got away from there as fast as I could, heaving a sigh of relief that I had made my call. I never went back a second time.

I was pitiful! Scared to do the right thing! And yet, I don't think that I'm the exception in Christianity. From what I've picked up in talking with others, most Christians are afraid to talk to others about the Lord. You're afraid someone won't like you, or you're afraid that they'll make fun of you, or you're afraid that you won't know what to say or . . . And so, instead of obeying the Lord's command to reach the lost by giving them the gospel, you keep quiet. You come up with the pious excuse that you are "letting your light shine" by the way you live. You are content that "everybody knows where you stand." You limit your soulwinning to praying for the lost. You say that God has called you to a different ministry—working in the nursery or singing in the choir or some other activity at church. Or you ask the pastor to talk to someone about the Lord that you have a burden for. The fact remains that most Christians do not win the lost to Christ. Most Christians do not even try to win the lost. Early in our nation's history, there was a popular frontier saying that described the people who failed to move west: "The cowards never started and the weak died by the way."[2] Sadly, that might be said of most Christians today.

Let me ask you a question. How many times has someone tried to win you to the Lord? If you're like most Christians, no one has ever spoken to you about the Lord. You should thank Him if you had godly parents who taught you about Christianity. Even in Christian families, that's rare. I'm over seventy years old and have never had anyone witness to me. The closest anyone has ever come to telling me about the Lord happened when I was a teenager. I was visiting at a church activity for young people. As a get-acquainted game, the visitors formed an inner circle and the regulars formed an outer circle. The piano played and the two circles walked in different directions until the music stopped. Then the regulars introduced themselves to the visitors. One man introduced himself and then said, "Are you a Christian?" I replied, "I don't know." He answered, "Well, I certainly hope you find out." That was it! It was his golden opportunity but he walked away from it. That led to a couple more wasted years until I later publicly declared my faith in Christ.

Christian leaders down through the ages have spoken of reaching others with the gospel. Augustine, the fourth-century bishop of Hippo, in northern Africa, wrote of his mother, "In the flesh, she brought me to life in this world: in her heart she brought me to birth in [God's] eternal light."[3] In the journal of Francis Asbury, a late eighteenth- and early nineteenth-century Methodist preacher, he wrote: "Little sleep last night. Let me suffer, and let me labour; time is short, and souls are daily lost."[4] Charles Spurgeon, pastor in London, wrote, "Even if I were utterly selfish, and had no care for anything but my own happiness, I would choose if I might, under God, to be a soul-winner; for never did I know perfect, overflowing, unutterable happiness of the purest and most ennobling order till I first heard of one who had sought and found the Saviour through my means."[5] Will Houghton, a former president of Moody Bible Institute in Chicago, said, "Your chief business on earth is to be a witness. In fact, it's your only excuse for living. If you are less than that, you are nothing. He saved you by His grace, and said, 'You are a witness.'"[6]

The Lord has given you the tools to do the job. He didn't leave you the command to evangelize but forget to give you the resources you need. And that's the purpose for this book. I want to remind you of several of the basic resources that will help you reach others with the gospel. There are basic resources for you to use, and there are basic practices for you to follow. The following pages will develop these areas for you. Someone has well said, "We have all eternity to tell of victories won for Christ, but we have only a few hours before sunset to win them."[7] By the grace of God, may you use the "few hours" left to you to tell others that Jesus Christ died to save them from their sin.

CHAPTER ONE

PREPARING TO USE THE RESOURCES

THE CALL TO EVANGELISM

WITHOUT LEAVING ROOM for any exceptions, the Lord has called every Christian to bring lost souls to Him. If you know Jesus Christ as your Savior, you have a divine commission to try reaching those who are unsaved with the gospel. The Lord said, "Herein is my Father glorified, that ye bear much fruit; so shall ye be my disciples. . . . Ye have not chosen me, but I have chosen you, and ordained you, that ye should go and bring forth fruit, and that your fruit should remain" (John 15:8, 16). Luke repeated this commission, "Ye shall receive power, after that the Holy Ghost is come upon you: and ye shall be witnesses unto me both in Jerusalem, and in all Judea, and in Samaria, and unto the uttermost part of the earth" (Acts 1:8). The world around you is rushing at top speed on a downhill path that ends in hell. The Lord is relying on you to turn around some of the people you meet.

Notice that I said above, "You have a divine commission to *try* reaching those who are unsaved with the gospel." It's important to recognize that the results of your efforts at witnessing are up to the Lord. Your responsibility is to "*try* reaching those who are unsaved with the gospel." The Lord's responsibility is to use your efforts to bring the lost to Himself. Of course, you should do the best you can as you witness to others. That's one of the purposes of this book—to help you become more effective in your soulwinning efforts. But it is God's responsibility to draw people to Jesus Christ. The Lord taught His disciples, "Therefore said I unto you, that no man can come unto me, except it were given unto him of my Father" (John 6:65). As you try to reach others, from time to time the Lord will use your witness to bring others to salvation.

In addition to His call to you, the Lord has given you resources to help you be effective in your witnessing. Before you can use these resources, however, you must answer His call to evangelism. The Lord has no other hands than your hands, no other voice than your voice, and no other eyes than your eyes. What He does, He must do through you and through others who respond to His call to evangelize the lost. The Lord could have written the gospel in flaming letters a mile high across the sky. He has not. Instead, He has chosen to use you and others like you to reach the lost with the message that "Jesus saves!"

The call of the apostles in the New Testament shows the pattern by which God calls people into His service. The Lord did not choose the twelve apostles to follow Him because they were people with special gifts He could use. No, as far as we know, they were average, down-to-earth people. At least four of the apostles were fishermen, one was a tax collector for the Roman government, and no vocation is associated with the rest of them. Logically, you would think that the Lord would have called the best of the best to serve Him. He would have called the wisest, the most skillful, the best speakers, the most talented, the wealthiest, and the most influential. But God's ways are not our ways and His thoughts are not our thoughts (cf. Isa. 55:8–9). He called people who gave no indication that they were exceptional.

The apostle Paul put it this way: "For ye see your calling, brethren, how that not many wise men after the flesh, not many mighty, not many noble, are called: but God hath chosen the foolish things of the world to confound the wise; and God hath chosen the weak things of the world to confound the things which are mighty; and base things of the world, and things which are despised, hath God chosen, yea, and things which are not, to bring to nought things that are" (I Cor. 1:26–28). Elsewhere, he said "But we have this treasure in earthen vessels, that the excellency of the power may be of God, and not of us" (II Cor. 4:7). You are one of the "earthen vessels" that the Lord wants to use to reach others with the gospel.

I think of a former student who struggled to make a C in one of my classes. A nice guy but very average in his grades. The Lord has used him for many years as a successful missionary. I think of another man with a below average IQ. God has used him greatly as the pastor of a large Baptist church. I know a man who graduated from college in the lower one-fourth of his class. He persevered in graduate school and taught in a Christian college. These examples can be multiplied many times. Bob Jones Sr. said, "The greatest ability is dependability." The Lord looks for willing servants, not for above-average people.

It is not that God can't use people with great talent. He can! There are many fine Christians who have well-developed skills and abilities they use for the glory of the Lord. But they are not fine Christians because of their gifts. They are fine Christians because they have dedicated themselves, their abilities, and their resources to the Lord. They have given all they are and all they have to Him. The Lord uses them to win others to Himself because they have committed themselves to Him. God works this way today. It makes no difference what talents you may have, what personality you may have, or what resources you may be able to bring to your efforts; the Lord wants to use you also to reach others with the gospel.

If the Lord used only people with sparkling personalities, exceptional gifts, and broad resources, everyone would give the credit to them for the success of Christianity. When God uses ordinary people or even people below average in their abilities and resources, it becomes clear that it is the power of God that is the reason for their success. Since the Lord is worthy to receive the glory, He carries out His work with people just like you. He looks for dedicated people who will freely submit to the leading of the Holy Spirit in their lives and people who are willing to put His work ahead of their own goals.

The important thing to note is not the ability of the person whom the Lord calls to evangelize others but that God calls every Christian to reach out to the lost. There are many things in the Bible that can't be misunderstood. We read a verse such as "These were more noble than those in Thessalonica, in that they received the word with all readiness of mind, and searched the scriptures daily, whether those things were so" (Acts 17:11). It is clear from this verse that God highly values Christians reading their Bibles. We read the Lord's statement "Give, and it shall be given unto you; good measure, pressed down, and shaken together, and running over, shall men give into your bosom. For with the same measure that ye mete withal it shall be measured to you again" (Luke 6:38) and see that Christians should support the Lord's work with their gifts. Verses such as "Rejoice in the Lord alway: and again I say, Rejoice" (Phil. 4:4) teach us that Christians should be joyful over spiritual things. And when we read "Go ye into all the world, and preach the gospel to every creature" (Mark 16:15), it is likewise clear that every believer should give the gospel to others. Bringing this home to you in your situation, you should give the gospel to the others that God brings across your path as you go through life. You have neighbors and coworkers that you see regularly. You have close family and relatives that you meet once in a while. You have friends and folks that you meet casually. When you consider the message given in Mark 8:36, "For what shall it profit a man, if he shall gain the whole world, and lose his own soul," you see the value that God has placed on the souls of men. Your divine calling to reach the lost with the gospel is the highest calling you can have.

THE PREPARATION OF A SOULWINNER

There are many ways of referring to the business of getting the lost to Jesus Christ. You may call it witnessing, testifying, personal work, fishing for souls, soulwinning, evangelism, reaching the lost, or something else. I once heard a sermon entitled "Frogging for Christ." The pastor had recently returned from a vacation in which he had been "frogging." He compared the steps in catching frogs to similar steps in reaching lost souls. It is not important what you call it. Going after the unsaved fulfills the Great Commission: "Go ye therefore, and teach [or 'make disciples of'] all nations" (Matt. 28:19). Like skills in other areas of life, it takes preparation to reach the lost with the message that Jesus Christ died for them.

One necessary step in developing your soulwinning skills is mental preparation. You must recognize that there is a need, a great need, an urgent need, a need that God has called you to meet, and a need that in all likelihood only you can meet. Without a personal relationship to God through Jesus Christ, men and women are lost spiritually. They are doomed to spend eternity in hell. All have sinned against the Lord and all face the penalty of hell for their sin. The vast majority of people in the world have never heard the gospel. Most people have never even heard the name of Jesus Christ, let alone the need to trust Him for their salvation. Unless someone tells them of Christ's sacrifice for them at Calvary, they will die and suffer lasting punishment.

"One of the characters in *Alice in Wonderland* is a lock . . . [who] was very restless. It could not be still even for a moment. It was always running around looking behind every stone, stump, and tree. It was always hunting for something. As Alice watched it, her curiosity was aroused, and she asked, 'What is the matter?' The lock replied, 'I am seeking for something to unlock me.'"[1] That's what the world needs—something to unlock them from the bonds of sin. You can be the one who unlocks others from their sinful bondage.

As you decide that you will meet this need, you must be certain of your own salvation. You need the assurance that God has saved you by the sacrifice of His Son at Calvary. You should know that your sins have been forgiven. The late Vance Havner said, "We take our faith for granted, and what we take for granted we never take seriously."[2] You need to take your salvation seriously. George Goodman, an early twentieth-century Bible teacher and preacher, put it this way: "A Christian without assurance of salvation is like a man walking in the dusk instead of the sunshine."[3] You must have the assurance that Jesus Christ has redeemed you from your sins.

It is next to impossible to convince another person of something you aren't certain of yourself. Several years ago, I spent my summertime selling Fuller Brush Company products door-to-door to folks I met in their homes. I spoke with a woman who was enthusiastic about the broom she had bought several years earlier from the company. She had used it first as a kitchen broom; then, when the bristles were showing a little wear, she bought another broom for the house and turned the worn one into her patio broom. By the time she showed it to me, the bristles were about two inches long, but it still served as the broom she used to sweep her concrete patio. As I went through the area, I told everybody about this woman who had used her Fuller Brush broom for well over twenty years. I could honestly encourage people to buy the brush products of the company because they were good products. I believed in them. On the other hand, the Fuller Brush Company also had a line of cosmetics for women. All I could do with the cosmetics was to offer them to my customers. I couldn't get enthusiastic about them since I didn't know that they were any better than cosmetics from other sources. What I believed in I could sell but what I wasn't sure of I could only tell people about. The same is true of your salvation. You need the certain knowledge that the gospel has changed your eternal future.

The assurance of your salvation comes from the Bible, from the Spirit of God, and from Christian living. As you read your Bible on a daily basis—and you need to have this kind of relationship to God's Word—it will increase your confidence in Christianity. I learned this years ago when I decided to see what the Bible had to say about assurance. As I read the New Testament, I marked verses that touched on the subject. It was clear that God's Word taught that we can have assurance of our salvation.

The Holy Spirit also witnesses to you of your salvation. "The Spirit [Him]self beareth witness with our spirit, that we are the children of God" (Rom. 8:16). "Now we have received, not the spirit of the world, but the spirit which is of God; that we might know the things that are freely given to us of God." (I Cor. 2:12). "Hereby know we that we dwell in him, and he in us, because he hath given us of his Spirit" (I John 4:13).

As you get to know God's Word better, you will get to know God better. You'll want to please the Lord by obeying the commands He has given. Unfortunately, most churches are filled with people who say they believe one thing but do another. They say that they believe in prayer but they don't spend much time praying. They say that they believe in giving but they don't give much of their money to the work of the Lord. They say that they believe in the local church but they don't attend regularly. Don't fall into the trap of patterning your Christianity after the Christianity you see in others. Make sure you don't fail the Lord by ignoring His Word and its commands. Above all, set out to obey the Bible's command to tell the lost about Jesus Christ and the salvation from sin that He offers.

As you put these simple principles into active practice in your own life, you will gain confidence that God's way is the right way. Perhaps I should put it this way: for Christians, God's way is the only way! Repeated over a period of time, the Bible, God's Spirit, and Christianity in action will increase your assurance of your own salvation. As you put your Christianity into practice in your daily life, you will also develop a greater love for the Lord, Who has saved you. Because you love Him, you will want to please Him. You please the Lord as you totally submit yourself to Him. Your submission to the Lord must be complete. It will involve everything you are and everything you have. It will involve your dreams and aspirations for the future. There is no such thing as a partial loyalty to the Lord. It is total loyalty or it is not loyalty at all.

You recognize this in human relationships. You would be highly upset if your husband or wife were only 99 percent faithful to you. That 1 percent unfaithfulness would ruin the relationship. You would be upset if your son or daughter obeyed you 99 percent of the time. You would punish them for their 1 percent of disobedience. You wouldn't be happy if your employees did their job only 99 percent of the time. You want 100 percent efficiency. The same is true of your faithfulness to the Lord. He wants you to be faithful 100 percent of the time.

The Lord told His disciples, "Follow me, and I will make you fishers of men" (Matt. 4:19). They responded by leaving their fishing nets and following Him. This was a decision of *the will*. The apostle Paul later urged the Roman believers, "Present your bodies a living sacrifice, holy, acceptable unto God, which is your reasonable service" (Rom. 12:1). This was a decision to give *the body* to the Lord. Paul followed this command by saying, "Be not conformed to this world: but be ye transformed by the renewing of your mind, that ye may prove what is that good, and acceptable, and perfect, will of God" (Rom. 12:2). This decision involved *the mind*. Elsewhere, Paul advised the Corinthian believers, "He which soweth sparingly shall reap also sparingly; and he which soweth bountifully shall reap also bountifully. Every man according as he purposeth in his heart, so let him give; not grudgingly, or of necessity: for God loveth a cheerful giver" (II Cor. 9:6–7). Giving involves your *possessions*. John wrote the well-known admonition, "Love not the world, neither the things that are in the world. If any man love the world, the love of the Father is not in him. For all that is in the world, the lust of the flesh, and the lust of the eyes, and the pride of life, is not of the Father, but is of the world. And the world passeth away, and the lust thereof: but he that doeth the will of God abideth for ever" (I John 2:15–17). This involves your *goals* and *ambitions*.

Your *will*, your *body*, your *mind*, your *possessions*, your *goals* and *ambitions*—you must give everything to the Lord. Your dedication to Jesus Christ involves everything you possess and everything you ever will be. Anything less than this is not dedication at all. Your love for Jesus Christ will result in giving yourself to Him. You will want to witness to others because you want them to have the same relationship with the Lord that you enjoy.

Your relationship to the Lord will give you the same kind of love for others that He has for them. His love led Him to give Himself so that sinful men would come to Him for salvation. Your love should lead you to give yourself to bringing others to the Savior. The Bible gives illustrations of this kind of love. "Oh that my head were waters, and mine eyes a fountain of tears, that I might weep day and night for the slain of the daughter of my people" (Jer. 9:1). "When [the Lord] saw the multitudes, he was moved with compassion on them, because they fainted, and were scattered abroad, as sheep having no shepherd" (Matt. 9:36). "Therefore watch, and remember, that by the space of three years I [Paul] ceased not to warn every one night and day with tears" (Acts 20:31). You need the same compassion that the Bible illustrates with these men.

The Holy Spirit will produce this love in you as you grow spiritually. According to Galatians 5:22–23, it is part of the ninefold "fruit of the Spirit." This includes "love, joy, peace, longsuffering, gentleness, goodness, faith, meekness, [and] temperance." It is not something you decide to add to your personality. It is not "worked up" by some actions that you take. It is the result of God's Spirit working in you as He prepares you for effective service for the Lord.

Do you have these qualifications? Do you understand that God has called you to reach others for Him? Do you see the need of others all around you? Are you sure of your own salvation? Do you love the Lord? Solomon wrote, "If thou faint in the day of adversity, thy strength is small. If thou forbear to deliver them that are drawn unto death, and those that are ready to be slain; if thou sayest, Behold, we knew it not; doth not he that pondereth the heart consider it? and he that keepeth thy soul, doth not he know it? and shall not he render to every man according to his works?" (Prov. 24:10–12). Are you seeking to fulfill your commission to win the lost? Or have you "faint[ed] in the day of adversity"? As you begin looking at the resources for success in soulwinning, be sure you have the mental preparation that will let the Lord use you for His glory.

The eighteenth-century British evangelist George Whitefield captured the attitude that believers should have when he wrote, "Believe me, I am willing to go to prison or death for you. But I am not willing to go to heaven without you."[4] That's the attitude that will cause you to sacrifice yourself as you look for opportunities to tell others around you that they can be saved by trusting the finished work of Jesus Christ.

CHAPTER TWO

THE GREATEST RESOURCE

THERE IS NO question but that the Bible teaches that Christians should bear spiritual fruit. "Even so every good tree bringeth forth good fruit" (Matt. 7:17*a*). "And he that reapeth receiveth wages, and gathereth fruit unto life eternal: that both he that soweth and he that reapeth may rejoice together" (John 4:36). "I am the vine, ye are the branches: he that abideth in me, and I in him, the same bringeth forth much fruit: for without me ye can do nothing. . . . Herein is my Father glorified, that ye bear much fruit; so shall ye be my disciples. . . . Ye have not chosen me, but I have chosen you, and ordained you, that ye should go and bring forth fruit, and that your fruit should remain: that whatsoever ye shall ask of the Father in my name, he may give it you" (John 15:5, 8, 16). "That ye might walk worthy of the Lord unto all pleasing, being fruitful in every good work, and increasing in the knowledge of God" (Col. 1:10). These and many other verses that could be added make it clear that God expects His children to bear spiritual fruit.

Three words relate to "fruit" in the New Testament.[1] Taken together, these occur eighty-three times. Seventeen of the books in the New Testament and twenty-nine of books in the Old Testament refer to "fruit." The four Gospels—Matthew, Mark, Luke, and John—mention *fruit*. The book of Acts mentions it. Eleven of the Epistles refer to fruit in some way. The first command after the creation of the world concerned the "fruit" of physical children (Gen. 1:28*a*). Although He did not use the word "fruit," it is appropriate that the last command of the Lord before His ascension into heaven concerned the "fruit" of spiritual children (Acts 1:8).

God has given you one resource to help in your soulwinning efforts that towers above every other possible resource that you might think necessary. God has given you the Holy Spirit to help you point others to Jesus Christ for salvation. The Holy Spirit gives you spiritual power in your witnessing. The prophet Micah illustrates this with his statement, "But truly I am full of power by the spirit of the Lord" (Mic. 3:8*a*). After His resurrection from the garden tomb, the Lord commanded His followers, "Behold, I send the promise of my Father upon you: but tarry ye in the city of Jerusalem, until ye be endued with power from on high" (Luke 24:49). He repeated the command just before His ascension up into heaven, "Ye shall receive power, after that the Holy [Spirit] is come upon you" (Acts 1:8*a*). Fifty days later, at Pentecost, God sent the Holy Spirit to empower believers for their service.

The apostle Paul relied on this power in his ministry. "Through mighty signs and wonders, by the power of the Spirit of God; so that from Jerusalem, and round about unto Illyricum, I have fully preached the gospel of Christ" (Rom. 15:19). "And my speech and my preaching was not with enticing words of man's wisdom, but in demonstration of the Spirit and of power" (I Cor. 2:4). "For God hath not given us the spirit of fear; but of power, and of love, and of a sound mind" (II Tim. 1:7).

If you have placed your faith in Jesus Christ as your Savior, this same power is available to you. Every Christian has the

Holy Spirit living in him. Paul stated this negatively, "But ye are not in the flesh, but in the Spirit, if so be that the Spirit of God dwell in you. Now if any man have not the Spirit of Christ, he is none of his" (Rom. 8:9). Later, he stated it positively, "In whom ye also trusted, after that ye heard the word of truth, the gospel of your salvation: in whom also after that ye believed, ye were sealed with that Holy Spirit of promise" (Eph. 1:13). The apostle John made this same point: "Hereby we know that he abideth in us, by the Spirit which he hath given us" (I John 3:24*b*).

I've seen the work of the Holy Spirit over and over in my own witnessing. While my wife and I were visiting a pastor friend and his wife in North Carolina, I went out with a man in the church to call on some prospects who needed salvation. We stopped at one house and spent thirty or forty minutes making absolutely no progress in reaching the man who lived there. He was not interested. As we left, I said to him, "John, the only reason that you don't get saved is that you're happy in your sin." Several months later, we visited again. When we reached the church, the pastor said, "Pete, I've got someone I want you to meet." You guessed it! There was John, now an active member of the church. He told me, "After you left, I couldn't get those words out of my mind. I was 'happy with my sin.' I went to bed and tossed and turned most of the night while thinking that I was 'happy with my sin.' For the rest of the week, I thought about being 'happy with my sin' and, the next Sunday, I went to church and got saved." Now, who gets the credit for that decision? I certainly didn't do anything special. The pastor didn't do anything special. No one else spoke to the man about his need to accept the Lord. But the Holy Spirit used a chance phrase, spoken without any special thought, to bring the conviction that led John to Christ.

In a very real sense, everyone who comes to Jesus Christ through your witnessing will come because the Holy Spirit draws him to the Lord. The New Testament makes this clear.

"No man can come to me, except the Father which hath sent me draw him: and I will raise him up at the last day" (John 6:44). The Old Testament puts it this way: "The Lord hath appeared of old unto me, saying, Yea, I have loved thee with an everlasting love: therefore with lovingkindness have I drawn thee" (Jer. 31:3). I've seen people weep with conviction as God's Spirit broke them with the knowledge of how terrible their sin was to God. The Holy Spirit works in the heart of a sinner to give him the desire to be saved: "No man can say that Jesus is the Lord, but by the Holy [Spirit]" (I Cor. 12:3*b*).

Your responsibility as a soulwinner is to not limit the work that God's Spirit wants to do through you. You limit Him generally in one of two problem areas. In the first place, many Christians continue to practice sin. Oh, you are selective in what you do. Hopefully, you have cleaned up your language, you probably don't get drunk or use drugs, and you don't beat your wife. But there are sins that most Christians don't think about twice. You still lose your temper. You are proud. You covet things that you can't afford to buy. You don't mind laughing at an off-color joke. You don't give your employer a full day's work. You make decisions without asking the Lord what He wants you to do. And I probably shouldn't even get started on the sins of omission that plague many Christians—failing to read their Bible, failing to pray, failing to give tithes and offerings to the Lord, failing to . . .

It is not that God can't work sovereignly through a backslidden Christian. God uses the resources that are available, and sometimes those resources are flawed. But your sin can limit God's ability to work through you. Israel's sin caused them to wander forty years in the wilderness of Sinai (Num. 14:26–35). The sin of Moses kept him from entering the Promised Land (Num. 20:12). The sin of Ananias and Sapphira brought them to a premature death (Acts 5:1–10). You should not boldly assume that God will overlook your sin just because you are witnessing to the lost.

The second problem involves the failure to dedicate yourself fully to the Lord. This reason underlies the first problem. You sin because you haven't given the Lord complete control of your life. You have the Holy Spirit in you, but you have not given Him the right to guide your life. This, by the way, is not a one-time decision. Acts 2:4*a* describes the filling of the Spirit in the early church: "They were all filled with the Holy [Spirit]." Just two chapters later, in Acts 4:8, Peter, "filled with the Holy [Spirit]," preaches to the Jews. In Acts 4:31, the Holy Spirit fills the early church again: "They were all filled with the Holy [Spirit], and they spake the Word of God with boldness." The first deacons of the early church came from men filled with the Holy Spirit (6:3, 5). Stephen, the first martyr, was "full of the Holy [Spirit]" (7:55). After his conversion, Saul was "filled with the Holy [Spirit]" (9:17). In his ministry later, the apostle Paul was again "filled with the Holy [Spirit]" (13:9). Barnabas was "full of the Holy [Spirit]" (11:24). The disciples were "filled [again] with the Holy [Spirit]" (13:52). Paul commanded the church at Ephesus to "be filled with the Spirit" (Eph. 5:18). There is only one salvation but there are many fillings of the Holy Spirit. You need His power today and you need His power tomorrow as well.

These examples are clear. You should yield yourself to the Lord every day, perhaps many times each day, as you ask the Holy Spirit to control you. When you do this, the Lord can do His work through you. On some days He will use you to bring a lost person to Himself. I recall a day that I had asked the Lord to use me. I was in San Diego when I saw a teenage boy hitchhiking. I stopped to pick him up, thinking that I might witness to him. Before I could start, he saw a friend and asked me to pick him up also. I did, and with their conversation going on, couldn't find a way to change the conversation to spiritual things. In just a few blocks I stopped to let the first boy out. Then, with only the second boy in the car, I was able to witness and lead him to pray the sinner's prayer. Again, who gets the credit for that decision? It was the Holy Spirit that brought him across my path. The Holy Spirit arranged time for a private conversation. He brought conviction into the boy's heart and the desire for salvation. I couldn't have planned it any better. He did His work through me, but He did the work.

The Holy Spirit brings conviction into the lives of lost sinners. The Lord taught this, "When he [the Holy Spirit] is come, he will reprove the world of sin, and of righteousness, and of judgment: of sin, because they believe not on me; of righteousness, because I go to my Father, and ye see me no more; of judgment, because the prince of this world is judged" (John 16:8–11). Lost people need to feel guilt for their sin so that they can see their need to turn to Jesus Christ for salvation. It is the convicting power of the Holy Spirit that leads a person to repent of his wickedness. You may be eloquent but your eloquence will not bring conviction. You may be persuasive but your persuasiveness will not bring conviction. You may be friendly but your friendliness will not bring conviction. You may have all the answers to all the questions that people ask, but your wisdom will not bring conviction. It is God's Spirit working in the heart of the sinner that produces conviction for sin.

The same is true when it comes to persuading the sinner to trust the Lord for his salvation. Your eloquence, your persuasiveness, your winsome personality, and your wisdom are all in vain unless the Holy Spirit works in the heart of others as you witness to them. As you are filled with God's Spirit, He does His work through you to draw sinners to Jesus Christ.

The Holy Spirit brings about the actual conversion of a lost person. Jesus taught Nicodemus, "Verily, verily, I say unto thee, Except a man be born again, he cannot see the kingdom of God." Nicodemus responded, "How can a man be born when he is old? can he enter the second time into his mother's womb, and be born?" The Lord answered the question, "Verily, verily, I say unto thee, Except a man be born of water and of the

Spirit, he cannot enter into the kingdom of God. That which is born of the flesh is flesh; and that which is born of the Spirit is spirit" (John 3:3–6). The Holy Spirit brings a lost person to the new birth.

The Holy Spirit wants to do His work through you. He wants to use you to witness to your family, your neighbors, your friends, your coworkers, and in casual meetings with others—perhaps a waiter, a telephone solicitor, a gas station attendant, or a store clerk. Will you yield yourself to His control? Will you turn from the sin that limits His work through you? Will you use this resource that God has given to let you fulfill the Lord's last command?

G. Campbell Morgan described the work of the Holy Spirit this way: "When I attempt to do what I can't do, then I do it in the power of the Spirit."[2] That's what you need as you witness to the lost. Humanly speaking, it is impossible for you to bring about a spiritual decision; but God's Spirit, working through you, can bring lost souls to a saving knowledge of the Lord.

CHAPTER THREE

THE NEGLECTED RESOURCE

Your responsibility to witness to lost people is not debatable. You have a divine mandate to try to bring others to Jesus Christ for salvation. Many Christians, however, feel inadequate for the challenge of persuading some lost person of his need to turn to Jesus Christ. There is a good reason for your feelings of inadequacy: You feel inadequate because you *are* inadequate—you are inadequate if you witness in your own wisdom and spiritual power. God does not want you to rely on yourself, your abilities, and your resources. In addition to His Holy Spirit He has given a second resource to help you carry out the "great commission" to win the lost. He has given you His inspired Word, the Bible, to teach you the principles you need as you reach out to the lost. You should become familiar with the Bible—getting an overview of the whole message, learning where key verses are, and learning what it teaches. As you do this, you will learn the elements of the gospel and the answers to common questions or objections and become more comfortable in speaking with others about the Lord.

Unfortunately, most Christians don't bother to read their Bibles, or, if they do, they are sporadic and casual in their approach. One afternoon my wife and I were visiting a particular home where a couple of times previously I had talked with the husband in the family. He was hardened against Christianity and I had gotten nowhere with him. I wanted the chance to speak with his wife and, on this afternoon, she was the only one home. I went through the plan of salvation with her. Although she didn't go to church anywhere and lacked the confidence that she was saved, she felt that she was already a Christian. She could remember asking the Lord to save her, so I switched to verses that would give her some assurance that she was saved. One of the verses I turned to was I John 5:12: "He that hath the Son hath life; and he that hath not the Son of God hath not life." I pointed out to her that eternal life comes from faith in the sacrifice of Jesus Christ at Calvary. If she trusted Him alone for her salvation, she could be assured that she had eternal life. She responded, "That's exactly what I need. Would you mark that verse for me in my Bible?" She got up, went into the front room to get her Bible, held it up, and blew on it before bringing it to me. From the kitchen, I could see a cloud of dust as she blew. That's the problem in many Christian homes. You leave your Bible to gather dust except when you pick it up to carry it to church.

If you are going to be successful in life, you must follow a plan and the rules that relate to your goals. When you build a home, you draw up a blueprint and then build it to that pattern. Inspectors come to see that you have followed the rules—plumbing, concrete, framing, electrical, heating and air conditioning, and so forth. If you want to raise a garden, you must plant the right seeds at the right time, spray, fertilize, water, perhaps thin the plants, and weed, before you can harvest. When you work on your car, you may need a motor manual or a parts list. When you cook, you follow a recipe for the ingredients and the instructions. Why should it be any different in the spiritual realm? In order to successfully carry out God's will for your life, you must follow the instructions that He has given you in the Bible. That's one of the reasons we have the Bible. In His wisdom, God knew that we would need His inspired guidance in order to be successful in our Christian service.

There are several steps to follow as you seek to develop your skill in using the resource of God's Word. As you repeat these steps over a period of time, you will grow in your ability to use the Bible effectively. You will learn how to present the Lord to others and how to answer questions they may have.

READING THE BIBLE

You should read your Bible regularly. Paul commended the believers in Berea, "These were more noble than those in Thessalonica, in that they received the word with all readiness of mind, and searched the scriptures daily, whether those things were so" (Acts 17:11). In his letter to Timothy, the apostle urged him to "give attendance to reading" (I Tim. 4:13). The Bible does not tell how much you should read. That's probably a good thing. Some folks read with difficulty while others read rapidly. The average difficulty level of the Bible is about that of a sophomore in high school. Parts of it are fairly easy to read. Other parts, however, are very difficult to read and understand. You should read your Bible according to that that is appropriate to your ability and opportunity. My grandmother read slowly, but, in her last years, she spent several hours each day reading her Swedish Bible.

There is a challenge in reading the Bible. Most people don't read books at all. Now you find yourself faced with the challenge of reading a book of between thirteen and fourteen hundred pages. That's a lot! Others who have gone before you have set an example for you to follow. Martin Luther, the great reformer, set a goal of reading his Bible twice each year. He said, "For some years now, I have read through the whole Bible twice every year. If you picture the Bible to be a mighty tree and every word a little branch, I have shaken every one of these branches."[1] It is no wonder that God used him to shake Europe for Christ! Francis Asbury, an early Methodist preacher, spent two hours each day in reading his Bible.[2] Catherine Booth, cofounder of the Salvation Army, read the entire Bible through eight times before she was twelve years old.[3] George Muller, used by the Lord to meet the needs of several thousand orphans, read his Bible through about two hundred times, "one hundred of which were on his knees."[4] During the latter years of his life, he read the Bible through four times each year.[5]

John Quincy Adams, the sixth president of the United States, said, "I have myself for many years made it a practice to read through the Bible once every year. . . . My custom is to read four or five chapters every morning, immediately after rising from my bed. It employs about an hour of my time, and seems to me the most suitable manner of beginning the day."[6] With all due respect to our former president, he read slowly. For an average reader, there are only four books in the New Testament that take more than an hour to read—Matthew, Luke, John, and Acts. To balance this, there are five New Testament books that you can read in less than three minutes each—Titus, Philemon, II and III John, and Jude. The books of Galatians, Ephesians, Philippians, Colossians, I and II Thessalonians, I and II Timothy, James, I and II Peter, and I John will take between five and fifteen minutes each. That leaves Mark, Romans, I and II Corinthians, Hebrews, and Revelation for you to read giving each one between twenty and forty-five minutes. Since the Old Testament is about twice as long as the New Testament, it will take twice as long to read.

In order to successfully read your Bible through on a regular basis, you should set a definite time for your reading. For most Christians, this will involve getting up a few minutes earlier. I know that's a sacrifice. (But if you didn't stay up late at night watching television programs, you wouldn't be so tired in the morning.) It's generally harder to read your Bible at night. You have things to do around the house, the children make too much noise, or you get interested in something else. Before you realize where the time has gone, you are sleepy. In general, the morning is better. If you get up a few minutes earlier than normal, it'll be quieter and you'll have more privacy. Whatever time you decide on, stick with it. My mother waited until dad was off to work and we had left for school. Then she would sit down and spend time reading her Bible. My dad, on the other hand, got up early and spent the better part of an hour reading the Bible and having a time of prayer. Each one had a time that worked.

I have often suggested two things to various Christians who were starting to read their Bibles regularly. First, read your New Testament through at least three times before you tackle the Old Testament. The New Testament is easier to read because it's more familiar to you. It's easier to get bogged down in the Old Testament. I learned this when I began the habit of reading my Bible. Like any book, I started at the beginning. Genesis was okay; I could follow the stories. Exodus and Leviticus weren't bad; they still had connected thoughts. But when I got to Numbers, I hit some rough going. So and so begat so and so, and he lived several years and died, so and so begat so and so, and he lived and died, and . . . you get the idea. I was getting nothing (that I could tell) from the reading. It was boring and I was ready to quit. Fortunately, I mentioned the problem to my father and he steered me to the New Testament. I found it easier reading. After I had read it several times, I went back to the Old Testament and finished that. I needed to gain some spiritual maturity and some general knowledge of Christianity before I was ready for the Old Testament. The knowledge of the New Testament that you gain by reading it several times will help you understand the Old Testament better.

The New Testament is also more practical for you because it deals with Christian living. Your spiritual growth will depend on your understanding and obeying the teaching in the New Testament. When you have problems that confront you or when you have questions about standards for believers, you'll find your answers in the New Testament. When you want help understanding some Bible doctrine, you'll find the guidance you need in the New Testament. The great teachings of the Bible about salvation, the church, and future events largely rest on the writings of the New Testament authors.

The second thing that I suggest is that you read a certain number of pages each day. Four pages a day will take you through the average New Testament in about three months. Reading a definite number of pages is a personal preference. Some will recommend reading a certain number of chapters each day, but chapters are of uneven lengths, as little as 2 verses (Ps. 117) and as long as 176 verses (Ps. 119). Some recommend reading some in the Old Testament and some in the New Testament. That's okay, except that some Bible reading schedules seem to have no rhyme or reason to them other than that they cover the whole Bible in a year. Since I tend to be methodical in what I do, reading a definite number of pages works for me. I looked up the number of pages in my Bible, divided it by 365, and came up with the need to read 3½ pages a day if I wanted to finish the Bible in a year. I started reading 4 pages a day. I figured that the extra half page was needed to take care of days when I forgot to set the alarm or was sick and couldn't read. After a while, I moved to reading 8 pages a day. For several years I read 16 pages each day, 12 in the morning and 4 at night. Now I'm back to reading 8 pages in the mornings but spending more time in Bible study. I still feel I need that regular refreshing by reading those books in the Bible that I've already read scores of times.

STUDYING THE BIBLE

Studying the Bible is not just for the pastor and the Sunday school teachers. Even those of you who do not hold a teaching or preaching position have a responsibility to study the Word of God. "Study to shew thyself approved unto God, a workman that needeth not to be ashamed, rightly dividing the word of truth" (II Tim. 2:15). Contrast that with the rebuke in Hebrews 5:12–14: "For when for the time ye ought to be teachers, ye have need that one teach you again which be the first principles [or the ABCs] of the oracles of God; and are become such as have need of milk, and not of strong meat. For every one that useth milk is unskilful in the word of righteousness: for he is a babe. But strong meat belongeth to them that are of full age, even those who by reason of use have their senses exercised to discern both good and evil." The author of the book of Hebrews gives one of the sternest rebukes in the Bible to the readers of his letter because they had failed to learn the teachings of God's Word.

You may want to look up all the verses on a certain topic and organize them into a logical arrangement. As a newly dedicated Christian, I did that on the topic of baptism. Later, I studied the subject of assurance of salvation by listing all the verses that touched on the subject. For several years I marked passages that dealt with the family and then organized them into categories. You may get interested in a particular book and write out your thoughts on the book as you read through it. You may find a verse that you don't understand, so you read some Bible study guide to explain it. Whatever you do, it is a part of your Christian growth to study the Bible. You will never master it. Men have spent lifetimes studying the Bible without exhausting its depths. An infinite God wrote it, so you shouldn't expect to understand it all in a few short years. "The Bible is simple enough so that a child may wade in it, but deep enough so that an elephant may drown in it." The more you study the Bible, the more you realize that you need to study it more. Sam Jones described the Bible by saying, "If I understood all about the Bible, I'd know that somebody that didn't have any more sense than I have wrote it."[7]

Many good resources are available to help you in your study of the Bible. There are good commentaries on the individual books and on the Bible as a whole. There are Bible dictionaries and encyclopedias, concordances to help you find verses that mention a particular word or phrase, books on a variety of Bible topics, doctrinal books, and Sunday school literature. A good fundamental Bible-preaching church is a must if you want to learn what the Bible says.

There are two things to keep in mind as you select some help for your study. In the first place, Satan is no dummy! He has men writing material that will lead you astray. Be careful what you rely on. A friend commented on how much she enjoyed reading a certain author. She was startled when I told her that he was liberal in his theology. He was easy to read but not easy to trust.

If you belong to a fundamental Bible-believing and Bible-preaching church, ask your pastor or a trusted Christian friend to recommend something to help in your studies. I recall visiting a family when the mother proudly showed me the Bible storybook she had bought for her young children. As I leafed through it, I found that it had been published by a cult. The very first story taught heresy. I suggested to her that I'd be happy to pick out a reliable book that I would trade her for the unreliable one.

In the second place, keep in mind that books are like girlfriends or boyfriends. To each his own! What one person likes may not be what the next person uses. An author's writing style and emphasis makes a world of difference. If possible, check out a book before you buy it for yourself. I once had a student who heard a preacher recommend Harry Ironside's writings. Without checking, he went to a Christian bookstore and bought a set of Ironside's commentaries on the Bible. After he got home and started reading them, he found that Ironside's approach to the Bible was not what he needed. Be careful or you'll waste your money on books that will sit on your bookshelves and never be opened. Your church library, your pastor, or a friend may loan you a book for a short time so that you can see if it meets your needs.

MEMORIZE VERSES

I feel strongly that one of the great weaknesses in the church today is the failure of Christians to learn from memory the great verses of the Bible. Some years back, I had a friend who was a Jewish rabbi. He told me that he knew as a child that he wanted to be a rabbi. By the time he was in high school, he had memorized the Old Testament . . . in Hebrew! That challenged me. If an unsaved Jewish teenager saw the need to memorize Scripture, how much more should those of us who have trusted Jesus Christ for our salvation commit His Word to memory!

Jeremiah found the value of knowing the Bible. He wrote, "Thy words were found, and I did eat them; and thy word was unto me the joy and rejoicing of mine heart: for I am called by thy name, O Lord God of hosts" (Jer. 15:16). There was a time when the prophet was tempted to quit. The people of the land scorned him. He was put into prison. He was depressed and decided to give up his prophetic ministry: "Then I said, I will not make mention of him, nor speak any more in his name. But his word was in mine heart as a burning fire shut up in my bones, and I was weary with forbearing, and I could not stay" (20:9). The memorized Word of God gave him the strength to continue. The psalmist likewise found value in memorizing Scripture: "Thy word have I hid in mine heart, that I might not sin against thee" (Ps. 119:11).

You need to learn these same values by getting God's Word inside you. Don't make the excuse that you can't memorize. You learn other things by heart. You know the phone numbers of people you call often, you know where they live, and you know the driving rules of your state well enough to pass a test. Memorizing Bible verses comes the same way—review, review, and then review some more. There is no easy way to memorize. You have to go over and over the material in order to learn it. You do this with some things without being conscious that you're reviewing, for example, the name of your neighbors or the cross street at the corner of your block, and you memorize these things. You have even done that with some Bible verses, ones that you have heard mentioned so often in sermons or Sunday school lessons that you have learned them by heart. You should set out to learn additional verses. Choose verses that you can use in witnessing—Romans 3:23; 5:8; 6:23; 10:9, 10, and 13. Add some verses that bless and encourage you. Find verses that answer questions you have had. Add memorization and review to your daily time with the Lord.

Some people put their verses on cards to carry with them. When they have a few spare minutes during the day, they pull out the cards and review. I can often review fifty to one hundred verses while I'm waiting in the doctor's office. I can go for a walk around the neighborhood and review verses as I walk. Quite often, people will put a verse on a card and place it where they will see it during the day—over the kitchen sink, on their desk at the office. This is good but there still needs to be some other time that you systematically review the other verses you have learned.

By the time she was ten or eleven years old, Fanny Crosby had memorized the Pentateuch, the four Gospels, many of the Psalms, and all the books of Proverbs, Ruth, and the Song of Solomon. By the age of fourteen, she had memorized the whole Bible.[8] Of course, she didn't have television to interfere with her memory work. Keep in mind that Fanny Crosby was blind! If a handicapped child could memorize such large amounts of Scripture, don't you think you can memorize a few verses?

Meditate on Verses

In the Bible, there are many references to meditation. "This book of the law shall not depart out of thy mouth; but thou shalt meditate therein day and night" (Josh. 1:8). "But his delight is in the law of the Lord; and in his law doth he meditate day and night" (Ps. 1:2). "I will meditate in thy precepts, and have respect unto thy ways" (119:15). Christians today, however, generally neglect the practice of meditating on God's Word. Your world moves at breakneck speed. There is never enough time to get done all that you want to do. You move so fast from one thing to the next that you don't take time to think about the Lord and His Word.

Contrast the practice today with that of John Bunyan, the author of *Pilgrim's Progress* and other helpful Christian books. Referring back to earlier years of his life, Bunyan said, "I was never out of the Bible, either by reading or meditation."[9] The dictionary defines *meditation* as focusing your thoughts on something, as reflecting on or pondering it. You can't do this while the radio or TV is blaring. You can't do this while you are talking with someone else. You can meditate only when you take a few moments out of the day to think about God and His Word. Some people do this while they drive back and forth to work. They can talk to themselves as they drive. I usually take a few minutes in my daily devotions to ponder some verse that I've read. I try to meditate on roughly a chapter of the New Testament every month although there may be other times that I spend time thinking about a verse. Whatever you do, you need to take the time to reflect on spiritual things.

Take a verse and explain it to yourself. Is it a command? Does it touch on some doctrinal truth? Now, apply the verse to your life. Does it relate to some activity in the Bible that you sometimes get involved with? Does it rebuke something that you do but know is wrong? Does it teach something that you practice and need to be encouraged with? Every verse is different, so the possibilities of meditation are endless. You may find that meditating on a verse leads one way today and a different way tomorrow. The Holy Spirit has a way of drawing out practical applications, one at a time, to meet the needs that you have at different times.

I find meditation at night helpful. At those times when I wake up in the middle of the night and have difficulty getting back to sleep, I find that meditation can help. I mentally quote some verse to myself. It may be a familiar passage such as Psalm 23 or a newer verse that I've been memorizing. As I lie in bed, I meditate on the verse. Sometimes, I'll spend quite a while working my way through the verse (or passage). But many times, I'll drop off to sleep before I've finished the first word. Focusing my mind on God's Word has a calming effect that helps me shut out the worries and frustrations of life that sometimes keep me awake. In either case, whether I finish meditating on the passage or drop off to sleep, I've gained something desirable.

OBEY THE BIBLE

God expects you to live up to what you know. "Take heed unto thyself, and unto the doctrine; continue in them: for in doing this thou shalt both save thyself, and them that hear thee" (I Tim. 4:16). It is the continuing in God's Word that will influence others. "Blessed is he that readeth, and they that hear the words of this prophecy, and keep those things which are written therein" (Rev. 1:3). God's blessing comes to those who read and hear and obey!

This is the key to a successful Christian life. There is a cliché that says, "What you are speaks so loudly I can't hear what you say." If you say one thing about the Bible but do another, who will believe you? Christianity is filled with people who say one thing and do another. Many Christians say that they believe in prayer but spend only seconds a day talking to the Lord. They say that they believe in missions, but they do not pray for missionaries or give to support them. They say that they believe in the church, but they find excuses not to get involved in its activities or to attend its services. Studying the Bible without putting it into practice can be dangerous. It can lead to a cold, dead, dry, do-nothing Christianity.

If you have a problem in this area, it is possible that you are not a Christian. Christianity is more than just joining a church. It is more than believing that Jesus Christ died for the sins of the world. Christianity rests on your personal relationship with the Lord. A boy may believe that a girl loves him, but they will never get married until he asks her to become his wife. In the same way, you may believe that Jesus Christ loves you, but He will not become your Savior until you tell Him that you are sorry for your sins and then ask Him to forgive you and to become your Savior. This is the essential first step to obeying the Bible.

Jim Elliot, one of the martyred missionaries to the Auca Indians in Ecuador, said, "Obedience is the expression of love to God. Obedience leads to knowledge. Obedience means that we live in God. And if we live in Him, our lives bear the stamp of Christ."[10] G. Campbell Morgan, the great expositor of the Bible, said, "Obedience is the one qualification for further vision."[11] Other Christian leaders echo what these men have said. You need to obey the teachings of God's Word. Dr. Robert T. Ketcham, long-time leader in the GARB, put it this way: "All that God wants from anybody is obedience. You may have a thousand talents and you may have all the education in the world . . . but you can have all of this and if you are not obedient, you are not going to accomplish very much out in life for Christ."[12]

THE BIBLE AND SOULWINNING

I have taken some time to emphasize your relationship to the Bible because it is such an important resource as you attempt to win the lost to Jesus Christ. You can present the steps that lead to salvation from the Bible. You can use it as you answer questions people ask. You can use it to stress points that are unique to your witnessing situation.

Keep in mind that God has invested His Word with spiritual power. The Spirit of God often uses the Word of God to bring conviction of sin to a person. Jeremiah wrote, "Is not my word like as a fire? saith the Lord; and like a hammer that breaketh the rock in pieces?" (Jer. 23:29). The author of Hebrews put it this way: "The word of God is quick, and powerful, and sharper than any twoedged sword, piercing even to the dividing asunder of soul and spirit, and of the joints and marrow, and is a discerner of the thoughts and intents of the heart" (Heb. 4:12).

I was with a group holding services onboard a Destroyer Escort that was in port. Some of the men could not go on liberty because of responsibilities they had, so we came to them to give them the opportunity to hear God's Word. The bosun's mate announced that religious services would be held in the mess hall, and several men came. I began talking with a young man and found that he was not saved. He had grown up in a liberal church where the pastor taught that God was going to save everyone. As we talked, I began casually flipping through Matthew. I showed him Matthew 5:22, "Whosoever shall say, Thou fool, shall be in danger of hell fire." Then I moved on to verses 29–30 in the same chapter, where it says twice, "It is profitable for thee that one of thy members should perish, and not that thy whole body should be cast into hell." Then we looked at Matthew 10:28, "Fear not them which kill the body, but are not able to kill the soul: but rather fear him which is able to destroy both soul and body in hell." Then I asked, "Does God send some people to hell?" The answer was obvious. He could see that the Bible taught that God punishes sinners with hell. And, seeing that, he could also see that he needed to trust

Christ in order to escape that punishment. The Bible did its work in bringing him to Jesus Christ for salvation.

God's Word also has the power to impart faith to those who believe it. The apostle Paul wrote, "So then faith cometh by hearing, and hearing by the word of God" (Rom. 10:17). As the lost hear God's Word, they are often brought to faith in Jesus Christ as their Savior. A. N. Groves, nineteenth-century missionary to India, wrote, "Remember our old rule, to judge according to God's word; let us be neither frightened nor allured from it . . . it will be the rock on which our battle with infidelity must be fought; therefore now learn to trust your sword, for it will cut deep if well wielded under the power of the Spirit."[13] Because it does "cut deep," you should learn it well so that you can use it effectively in your witnessing.

On one occasion as I preached in jail, a teenager named Charles responded to the invitation and I led him to the Lord . . . I thought. Afterwards, I told some of the other men who had come with me about the decision that Charles had made. One of them responded, "I led him to the Lord last week." I knew what had happened. Charles was in jail where he did not have the best surroundings. Something happened during the week, Charles got mad, probably swore at someone else, knew that he had sinned, and so thought that he needed to get saved again. I went to the same cell the next week, preached, gave an invitation, and Charles came forward again to be saved . . . for the third straight week. I went through the steps that lead to salvation and Charles prayed. This time, I stressed to him that if he had Christ, he had salvation. We went to I John 5:12, "He that hath the Son hath life; and he that hath not the Son of God hath not life." Charles couldn't read, so I repeated the verse over and over while he repeated it back to me. He had a speech impediment and couldn't say the short *a* after the *h* sound. So when he said the verse, it came out, "He that hayth the Son hayth life, and he that hayth not the Son of God hayth not life." I emphasized over and over that his salvation depended on what Christ had done for him. He was saved by his faith in Jesus Christ, not by what he did.

A week later I came back to the same cell. This time, I began by asking the men, "I'd like to know if there is anyone in the cell that is a Christian." Charles raised his hand. I asked him, "Charles, how do you know that you're saved?" He began, "He that hayth the Son hayth life," and I interrupted him with a hearty "Amen!" Charles had learned that salvation rested on having Jesus Christ. God's Word had done its work of giving him faith in the Lord. God's Word has the power to save. In I Peter 1:23, the apostle says, "Being born again, not of corruptible seed, but of incorruptible, by the word of God, which liveth and abideth for ever." Human reasoning can't save you. Philosophy can't save you. Good works can't save you. Money can't save you. Nothing can bring salvation except God's Spirit working to bring faith through God's Word to a lost person. Many people have found Jesus Christ through hearing God's Word as it is preached, either in church, on a street corner, over the radio, or in some other place. Many have found Christ as their Savior through God's Word presented in a gospel tract. Many people have found the Lord when a friend guided them through verses in the Bible that explain salvation.

I was preaching in jail and noticed a man sitting in front with tears streaming down his face. When I gave the invitation, he remained seated, giving no other response to what I had said. When the service was over, I engaged him in conversation. His name was Joe. When I asked him to respond to the gospel, he replied, "Preacher, God doesn't want me. I've sinned too much." When I dug a little deeper, I found that while he was in jail, his mother had died. He couldn't go to her funeral since it was in another state. The jail, however, arranged a phone call for him to his father. When his father came on the line, he told his son, "Joe, you have killed your mother by the life you have lived." Joe was subject to epileptic seizures. That night, he had an emotional reaction to the situation. He kept the jail awake as time after time, the guards had to bring medical help to him as he went through seizure after seizure. I showed up the next day to preach when Joe was caught up with the enormity of what he had done and its effect on his mother.

I came back a week later and preached on Psalm 51, the penitential psalm in which David recalls his actions that have led to "bloodguiltiness" (Ps. 51:14), the murder of Uriah and other unnamed soldiers. Joe did not respond. The following week, I preached from Psalm 32, a companion psalm to Psalm 51. This time, Joe opened his heart to the Lord. God's Word did its work in drawing him to accept Jesus Christ as his Savior.

God wants you to learn His Word so that you can use it as you witness to others. You will use your Bible to go through the steps that lead to salvation. There will be times that you will turn to a verse to answer some question that has been asked. There will be other times when you will make a point based on some verse. The Bible, God's inspired Word, is a tool you can't afford to be without as you obey the Lord's last command.

John Jasper was a slave in Virginia when he was converted. He later became a pastor and was used by the Lord to reach many with the gospel. Jasper said, "I take my stan' by de Bible an' rest my case on wat it say. I take wat de Lord says 'bout my sin, 'bout my Savior, 'bout life, 'bout death, 'bout de world to come. . . . Think dat I will fersake de Bible? It is my only Book, my hope, de arsnel uv my soul's surplies, an' I want nuthin' else."[14] Jasper did not have many of the advantages that most Christians have today, but he had the right attitude on God's Word. May God give you that same trust in the infallible Book.

CHAPTER FOUR

THE RESOURCE THAT'S
ALWAYS AVAILABLE

GOD HAS GIVEN every Christian a powerful resource to take with him wherever he goes. That means that you personally have this resource. It doesn't take up any space, doesn't have any weight, doesn't require any special training to use, doesn't cost you anything, and yet it has a value far beyond any dollar amount you can place on it. It is available to you night or day seven days a week, at home or at work, in your car or while you walk. The resource is prayer. You have the right of prayer and the privilege of prayer.

You can commit to the Lord your efforts to persuade others to repent of their sins and to trust the finished work of Jesus Christ at Calvary as the only thing that God will ever require for their sins. You can pray that the Lord will guide you to the right people, that He will help you make good contacts with those people, and that He will bring conviction in the hearts of those to whom you witness. You can pray that He will help you present the gospel clearly to those to whom you witness. You can pray that He will lead lost people to see their spiritual needs. You can pray that He will give you wisdom for the questions you answer. You can pray for specific people that God has burdened you to see come to Jesus Christ. You can pray about any situation you face as you try to point others to Christ. There is no limit to the number of things you can pray about as you try to bring lost people to the Lord.

The New Testament has many precious prayer promises: "And all things, whatsoever ye shall ask in prayer, believing, ye shall receive" (Matt. 21:22). "Hitherto have ye asked nothing in my name: ask, and ye shall receive, that your joy may be full" (John 16:24). "Therefore I say unto you, What things soever ye desire, when ye pray, believe that ye receive them, and ye shall have them" (Mark 11:24). "And whatsoever ye shall ask in my name, that will I do, that the Father may be glorified in the Son. If ye shall ask any thing in my name, I will do it" (John 14:13–14). "If ye abide in me, and my words abide in you, ye shall ask what ye will, and it shall be done unto you" (John 15:7).

The New Testament mentions prayer about three hundred times. Twenty-three of the twenty-seven books mention it in some way. Only Galatians, II Peter, and II and III John fail to mention prayer. God has given these promises to you as an encouragement to help you to pray. Certainly, a matter as important as the salvation of a lost soul is something you should bring to the Lord in prayer.

There are only two problems with using this resource. The first is a lack of faith that God answers prayer. I know that most Christians would never admit that they lack faith in the Lord. From a practical standpoint, however, most Christians act as though they don't have faith because most Christians don't spend a lot of time praying. I know that many Christians in fundamental circles spend more time in prayer than most other religious people, but I'm not sure that every fundamental Christian spends much time praying. Many Christians go throughout the week without often bowing their head to the Lord in prayer. My wife and I once spent several days on a cruise. A pastor and his wife ate at our table of eight every evening . . . without once bowing their heads to thank the Lord for the food. That's extreme, but many Christian are not much better. The attendance at the average prayer meeting in the average church shows the lack of concern many Christians have with prayer. There is a cliché that says, "Little prayer, little power; more prayer, more power; much prayer, much power." If you want power in your witnessing, you need to pray.

The second problem with getting answers to your prayers is sin. The psalmist well pointed out, "If I regard iniquity in my heart, the Lord will not hear me" (Ps. 66:18). Solomon commented, "The Lord is far from the wicked: but he heareth the prayer of the righteous" (Prov. 15:29). The New Testament teaches the same truth: "Now we know that God heareth not sinners: but if any man be a worshipper of God, and doeth his will, him he heareth" (John 9:31). Unchecked sin will keep you from getting answers to your prayers.

When I speak of sin, I'm thinking not only of sins of commission—drunkenness, cursing, stealing, and other obvious sins—but also of the sins of omission that so often hinder your Christian life. The failure to read your Bible regularly, the failure to rejoice in the Lord, the failure to be active in your local church, the failure to give tithes and offerings to support God's work, and many other sins of omission plague Christians today. You need to be totally committed to the Lord all the time.

Let me make it clear that I'm not speaking of sinless perfection. While that should be the goal of every Christian, all of us fail. You do something impulsively and have to ask the Lord's forgiveness. You do something ignorantly and find later that it was wrong. You misjudge a situation and commit some sinful act. As you walk with the Lord over a period of time, you'll gain the victory over sin more and more often. You'll have to fight against your sinful nature for the rest of your life. The key is that you are fighting it. You haven't given in. You haven't accepted certain sinful habits as all right. You haven't let the world dictate the standards you will follow.

When you pray, you bring the Lord into your life. When you commit the day to Him, you are asking Him to guide you in the various situations you'll face. When you pray about specific matters, you recognize His power to meet your individual needs. When you pray, you are obedient to His Word, and when you fail to pray, you are disobedient to it. That's why you should pray about everything, the minor matters in life as well as the major issues and decisions you face.

Prayer is absolutely necessary in your soulwinning efforts. Remember, whatever success you have in bringing a person to Christ comes because the Holy Spirit has worked in that person's heart. When you pray, you recognize the importance of the Spirit's work. You can't always create the opportunity to witness, but the Holy Spirit can. You can't bring a lost person to feel conviction over his sin, but the Holy Spirit can. You can't make a sinner respond to the gospel, but the Holy Spirit can. Your prayers invite the Lord to do the work through you that He wants to do.

During an overnight stay in a motel in the Midwest I went to the motel office to give the woman at the counter a gospel tract. We struck up a conversation about spiritual things. She was willing to talk about her lost condition, but another customer came to check in, so we abandoned the conversation. I hung around the office until she had finished with the customer, intending to pick up the conversation, but as that customer went out, another one came in. I breathed a silent prayer to the Lord, "Please keep any more customers from coming in." After she had registered the customer and assigned him to a room, I was able to start the conversation again. After explaining the gospel to her, I led her to ask the Lord to save her and spoke with her briefly about getting into a good church and steps that would help her grow spiritually, and then customers started coming in again. God gave me about fifteen minutes so that I could finish presenting Christ to her.

I had a similar situation at a local doughnut shop. I stopped there about six a.m. for a cup of coffee and a doughnut and was the only customer. The woman at the counter was willing to talk so I was able to bring up the gospel. As we talked, I mentally asked the Lord to keep customers away until we had finished. After I had explained the gospel to her, led her to pray that the Lord would save her, and briefly spoken about Christian growth, the customers started coming in. I've been in for doughnuts often at that time of the morning and have never seen that place empty of customers. That day, however, the Lord graciously worked to give me the opportunity of pointing the woman to Christ.

It would be nice if the Lord answered every prayer immediately. It doesn't work that way. The Lord has His timetable and it is up to you to adjust your schedule to it. Quite often, the Lord lets you pray and pray and pray. You should remember that Matthew 7:7 is in the present tense: "Ask, and it shall be given you; seek, and ye shall find; knock, and it shall be opened unto you." What it means is "keep on asking, and it shall be given you; keep on seeking, and you shall find; keep on knocking, and it shall be opened unto you."

I prayed daily for my brother's salvation for twenty-four years. During that time, I witnessed to him when the opportunity came along and got absolutely nowhere. But the Lord was working, bringing him to the point where he was ready. When he finally trusted the Lord as his Savior, it was in response to a small church near where he lived. The men of that church came by my brother's house on door-to-door visitation. My brother was impressed with the men and made his decision to attend their church and later accepted the Lord. I rejoiced over the answer to my prayers even though I wasn't there at the time of his salvation.

God answers prayer. If you want to win the lost to Him, you need to pray about your witnessing efforts. You should pray for specific unsaved people with whom you have contact.

Most of you have family members who are unsaved. You probably have neighbors, friends, and coworkers who are unsaved. Often unplanned opportunities will let you tell others about the Lord—a waiter, a parking lot attendant, or a store clerk. Someone may stop by and comment on your yard while you're working outside. Pray that the Lord will guide you through each day to be ready to reach out to others with the gospel. Pray for opportunities to witness. Pray about activities you may be involved with—a Sunday school class, a youth ministry, a local rest home or rescue mission, having folks over for dinner or dessert so that you can help them spiritually, a ball team that you coach, a community organization that you are involved with, or a thousand other activities. You should rely on the resource that Christians so often forget as you try to carry out the Lord's last command.

"At one time [in the life of the early Methodist preacher Francis Asbury], it was his practice to set apart three hours of every twenty-four for [prayer]; at another period in his life he gave himself to private prayer seven times a day; at another time it was his habit to spend a part of every hour when awake praying; at still another, ten minutes of every hour."[1] Pastor James Bryan of Birmingham, Alabama, spoke of the value of prayer for a pastor: "The pastor must live on his knees. He must advance on his knees. He must visit on his knees. He must prepare to preach on his knees. . . . The conditions of answered prayer are faith, a life with the sins forgiven, and the unselfishness which would not use the gift of prayer to satisfy an unworthy desire."[2] Mary Slessor, a missionary to Calabar, in Africa, likewise recognized the need for prayer. "Prayer is the greatest power God has put into our hands for service. Prayer is harder work than doing . . . but the dynamic lies that way to advance the kingdom."[3] These Christian workers have found the secret power that's available through prayer. Won't you join them in praying for the lost that God brings across your path?

CHAPTER FIVE

THE PRINTED RESOURCE

W HEN ROSA ELENA, of Opodepe, Mexico, was thirteen years old, she asked her mother several times, "How can I go to heaven?" Not having an answer, her mother simply told her to ask the nuns associated with the village church. She did but they could give her no help. After visiting some Christian friends in a nearby village, they gave her some clothes and a gospel tract. When she reached home, she went into her bedroom, read the tract, and trusted Jesus Christ as her Savior. Later, her mother and father were also saved.[1]

Kenny was without a church. A Jehovah's Witness invited him to attend one of their meetings. He received a gospel tract from a missionary and instead of attending the meeting of the Jehovah's Witnesses went to the small Bible study held by the missionary and began regularly attending. After some time, he accepted the Lord as his Savior.[2] A team of high school students spent a week in Brooklyn in a variety of activities as they supported the services at a local church. A few days after returning, Paul Levin, of Bible Tracts, Inc., wrote some of the students. He told them of a signed salvation decision slip that had come from a man who had received a tract from students on the subway.[3]

A study of students at Bob Jones University showed that slightly less than one percent had been converted directly on the basis of reading a gospel tract. Twenty-eight percent of these same students, however, said that a tract had been influential in bringing them to the point of salvation.[4]

I was going with a group on door-to-door visitation, inviting people to church and, as opportunity presented itself, talking with them about the Lord. When I reached Jason's door, no one was home. I left an invitation to our church and a gospel tract at his door and went on. The following Sunday, he came to the church and went forward at the invitation to receive Christ as his Savior.

These few stories illustrate the power of a gospel tract. Literature has a potential that most people do not pay much attention to. Ben Franklin said, "Give me twenty-six lead soldiers [letters for setting type], and I will conquer the world."[5] Martin Luther circulated his religious writings by means of several hundred thousand pamphlets throughout Europe. John Calvin, John Wesley, and many others from the time leading up to and on through the Reformation circulated copies of their tracts, books, miscellaneous religious writings, and sermons, which were a great help to the people who read them. This variety of religious literature helped to increase the spiritual level of the people and kept the Reformation growing. Luther and the other reformers could be in only a few places speaking to a few people, but their literature reached throughout the whole continent of Europe.

Other groups have learned the potential of literature. A nephew of Mahatma Gandhi said, "The missionaries have taught us to read, but the Communists have given us the literature."[6] Nicolai Lenin said, "Every Communist is to be actively engaged in the distribution of atheistic literature."[7]

The gospel tract offers you a simple but powerful aid to your witness for Christ. Bible Tracts, Inc., defines the tract as "a short, simple presentation of the Gospel message, printed in convenient pocket size, designed for easy distribution and use."[8] Most fundamental churches and Christian bookstores are a source of tracts for you to use as you try to reach the lost with the message that Jesus Christ wants to save them. You can also order tracts by means of the Internet or from national companies.

Advantages of Tracts

Aid to Conversation. There are many advantages to using gospel tracts. In the first place, a tract can be a conversation piece. When you give the tract, you can say something like "Here is something that can help you spiritually" or "Let me leave you this tract; it has a good gospel message in it" or "Here's a message you might enjoy." If the person reads it then, you can ask when he finishes if he has any questions or what he thought of the message. You can ask directly if he has ever made a decision to trust Jesus Christ as his Savior. The tract may serve as a springboard to let you present the steps of the plan of salvation.

Aid to Witnessing. A gospel tract can help you in your witnessing. One study has showed that about one person comes to Christ for salvation for every one thousand tracts that are distributed. Some tracts are organized in such a way that they help you in witnessing. I've seen several tracts that go step by step through the plan of salvation. If you are a Christian who does not have much experience in witnessing to others (or even one who has some experience), you can simply go page by page through the tract as you speak with someone about the Lord. Several years ago, I introduced one of these tracts in a high school chapel. Each student had a tract at his seat so he could follow along as I went through the tract. I had extra tracts at the door and invited the students to take as many as they needed. A couple of weeks later, one of the boys stopped by the office to let me know that he had led a friend to Christ by using the tract. He was not a spiritual leader in the school, but he had found an approach that worked for him in witnessing to others away from school.

My wife and I were traveling north on a business trip, and I stopped at a convenience store to fill up the tank with gas and gave a tract to the clerk. She was willing to talk so I began to give the plan of salvation to her. Some customers came in and I had to stop the conversation. I asked her to read the tract and then went on my way. Two or three weeks later, we were traveling along the same road on another business trip. I made it a point to stop at the same store. I got there just as the lady finished her shift. We went outside and I began to talk with her about the Lord. She told me that she was already a Christian. When I asked when she had made that decision, she related the story. She had kept my tract. When she went home after work that night, she sat on the bed and read the tract, then asked the Lord to save her. The tract had led her to receive Jesus Christ.

A Continuing Message. A gospel tract is a written message that continues to speak to people after you have gone. The person you have spoken with may forget what you have said, but when he picks up the tract, the message is still there to speak to him. I have read of cases in which a gospel tract brought someone to Christ as much as ten years after having first been given. Personally, I've been contacted six months later after speaking with a man and leaving a tract for him with my name and phone number on it.

Available in Many Languages. There are good gospel tracts available in many foreign languages for you to use. As you have the opportunity to travel in a foreign country, you can give a gospel witness by passing out tracts in that language. I can't speak Spanish or Italian or German or Russian, but I've been able to witness to people in countries where those languages are spoken. Quite often, as I'm involved in door-to-door visitation for church, I encounter people who don't speak English. There are enough Spanish-speaking people in the city where I live that I always have some Spanish tracts with me. We can't have much of a conversation but I can still be sure they have the gospel.

Convenient Size. Most gospel tracts are small and relatively easy to carry. They can fit inside your shirt or coat pocket or in your purse. They can fit inside an envelope. You can carry them in the glove compartment of your car. You should try to always have some gospel tracts with you or conveniently available. You never know when an opportunity to witness will come along, so you should be ready by having tracts to give out. Their convenient size makes this a possibility for you.

Designed for Different Purposes. While the gospel tract is primarily a tool for evangelism, different tracts take different approaches to presenting the gospel. These different slants let them meet the wide variety of needs that exist. For instance, I carry with me tracts written from a Catholic Bible. Some Roman Catholics will not trust a Protestant Bible, but they will read tracts with the verses taken from their Bible. I carry with me tracts that aim at Jehovah's Witnesses. I carry tracts written for children. I use tracts written to reach out to Jewish people. All these tracts present the gospel but they present it for different readers.

You can carry tracts with you that have been designed for special uses and seasons of the year. There are gospel tracts that have been written for hospital evangelism, for witnessing in jail, for ministries to children, for use with the military, and for other special ministries. There are tracts written for special times of the year—Easter, the Fourth of July, Halloween, Thanksgiving, and Christmas, as well as for those times when politicians are running for office. You can carry these with you at the appropriate times during the year. When the opportunity arises, you are ready to give them away.

Inexpensive to Use. A gospel tract is relatively inexpensive. Your church can often purchase a thousand of them for less than one hundred dollars. The price will vary depending on the quality and length of the tract. If you purchase tracts personally at your local Christian bookstore, you'll pay a little more because you won't get the quantity discount. The tracts will still be inexpensive. When you compare giving away one thousand tracts to what it costs to build church buildings and pay pastoral salaries, you see that the cost of a gospel tract is very reasonable. Tracts are an affordable aid to your witnessing.

Usable by any Christian. Any Christian can give out tracts. Not every Christian feels comfortable teaching a Sunday school class or going on church visitation. Not every Christian can preach at a local rest home or rescue mission. Many Christians don't feel comfortable working with children. But every Christian can give out a tract. This makes it possible for every believer to witness to the lost. Peter Cartwright, a Methodist circuit riding preacher and evangelist said, "It has been a question that I shall never be able to answer here on earth whether I have done the most good by preaching or by distributing religious literature. For more than fifty years I have firmly believed it was part and parcel of a Christian's sacred duty to circulate religious literature. I have spread thousands of dollars' worth among the reading public, sometimes a thousand dollars' worth a year. The religious press is destined, under the order of Providence, to minister salvation's grace to the perishing millions of the earth."[9] When you consider that Peter Cartwright ministered in the last half of the nineteenth century, when prices for literature were much less than today's prices, he must have given away several thousand gospel tracts and booklets each year.

Prepares You to Witness at Any Moment. When you carry gospel tracts with you, you can witness at any time an opportunity presents itself. One morning as I entered a doughnut shop, the waitress said, "How are you today?" I replied, "Wonderful."

Immediately, she cupped her hands together in front of her and said, "Could you give me some of that?" Yes, I could. I took out a gospel tract and put it in her hands. It wasn't convenient to speak with her since there were several customers, but I was able to give her the gospel that she could read later. You are not always planning to witness when you go into a store. Often, however, an opportunity will present itself to give a tract to a clerk or cashier. I try to give tracts to toll booth collectors or parking lot attendants, to gas station attendants, to waiter staff, to clerks in department stores, and to others as I have opportunity. You'll find many occasions when you can hand out a tract to someone, even when you weren't particularly planning to witness. When the chance to witness presents itself, having tracts with you lets you take advantage of the moment.

Enters Closed Doors. The gospel tract makes it possible for you to reach those whom circumstances keep you from reaching personally. For instance, you may do some business with a company by mail. You can enclose a gospel tract with your letters. For many years, I've sent gospel tracts with those bills I paid by mail. I've witnessed to people in Australia and Great Britain and Mexico who I've never seen. There are countries around the world that are closed to missionaries, but tourists or business travelers can give out tracts judiciously as they visit these countries. There may be a neighbor whose schedule is so different from your schedule that you never see him. A gospel tract with your name on it will let him know that you are interested in him. The gospel tract can take you behind the doors that are normally shut to the gospel.

Lets Others Know Where You Stand. Why not pick up a few tracts from your church and give them to your neighbors? You can invite them to church at the same time you give them the gospel. If you own or manage a business, place an attractive display of tracts by the cash register. Label the display "Free! Please take and read." Give a tract to your friends at work and try to develop a conversation about spiritual things. Keep tracts with you for those unexpected witnessing opportunities.

CHARACTERISTICS OF GOOD TRACTS

Not all tracts are created equal! Some tracts are written by professionals and have good organization and a lavish use of color and photographs. Some tracts emphasize the gospel, and other tracts emphasize religion. Some tracts are interesting, and some are boring. Some tracts are attractive, and other tracts are dog-eared and unattractive. You should choose those tracts that will make the best impression on the people whom you are trying to win to the Lord. An attractive gospel tract may cost a few cents more but is well worth the extra cost. You represent the King of Kings. What you do should reflect well on Him and on the Christianity that He offers to mankind.

Emphasizes the Word of God. An effective tract will stress God's Word in some way. It may do this by organizing several verses of Scripture to present some theme, usually the gospel. It may also do this by weaving verses into an interesting story or illustration that will attract people to read it. People write tracts for all kinds of reasons. You should make sure that the tracts you use present Christianity from a biblical viewpoint.

I avoid tracts that stress some scriptural truth that is not essential to salvation. I believe in baptism but I don't pass out tracts that emphasize it. I reserve things of this sort for private counseling as I guide a new believer into his or her steps of Christian growth. I believe in the local church but I don't think a tract should stress that alone. Literature from your local church should let people know what it believes about the gospel along with information about the church. I believe in tithes and offerings but I don't pass out tracts with a message that deals with giving. Let your tracts emphasize salvation. That is the greatest need people have.

Attractive Appearance. The tracts that you use should visually appeal to people. To this end, you should use gospel tracts that have an attractive appearance. Color is helpful—although, if you print your own tracts, make sure that the color combinations are easily read. I've seen tracts, for instance, with green or red type printed on white paper that are difficult to read. Pictures or photographs, especially on the front page of the tract, draw the attention of a person.

The tracts you use should have readable type. Some fonts are better for this than others. In these days when computers offer you a choice of hundreds of different types of fonts, be careful that you don't use one that is too small or too difficult to read. Many fonts are cute and attractive if you use them for a few words. They are counterproductive when you use them for a longer paragraph. The tract should be printed on good quality paper, not on newsprint. There should be a good layout to the blend of titles, photographs, illustrations, text, and so forth. These things are beyond the ability of most lay people, and, in most cases, the production of a tract should be left to a professional graphic designer.

Keep your tracts in good condition. If you carry them in your pocket, they will tend to get dog-eared and may get rain-spotted or dirty. Many Christian bookstores sell tract holders, a flexible plastic holder for tracts designed to fit into your pocket. It will wear out in a couple of years, but it will keep your tracts in better condition than if you simply put them in your pocket. You can make a tract holder from a manila file folder and some strong tape. This will serve to meet a temporary need but will not last more than a couple of months. It's worth spending a couple of dollars for the commercial product.

Interesting Title. The title of a tract should interest and challenge the reader. Most readers are indifferent to spiritual things. If the title attracts them, they may open the tract and begin reading. Modern business knows the value of a title. The Standard Oil Company spent millions of dollars changing the names of gas stations from Esso to Exxon. Automobile companies will research the names of their cars to find one that captures the attention of the public. They well remember the Edsel fiasco. The same is true of virtually every new product that comes to the stores—the manufacturer has chosen the name carefully. The same should be true with a gospel tract.

The Contents. An effective gospel tract should have contents that are interesting and persuasive. There will often be a highly readable story or a description of some natural phenomenon or the historical record of some event. The tract may take advantage of some current newsworthy event in the world that has been featured by the media. These contents aim to capture the reader's attention. The gospel message is either worked into the story or naturally follows it. Quite often, the tract will end with a decision form. The form encourages the reader to complete the form and mail it to an address. Often, there will be an offer of additional materials to help a person grow spiritually.

Although most tracts are relatively short—four pages is the norm—longer tracts are generally more effective in reaching people with the gospel. One study showed that every tract that had reported results of one thousand or more decisions was over six pages long. The tract "What Must I Do to Be Saved?" by John R. Rice is twenty-four pages long. Paul Levin's tract, "The New Birth," is eight pages long. Alexander Marshall wrote a tract, "God's Way of Salvation," that has been translated into at least eighteen foreign languages and has had millions distributed. The tract has two editions, twenty-four and thirty-two pages respectively.[10] These longer tracts can go into the gospel thoroughly. Shorter tracts have a place. They cost less to produce and can therefore be distributed more widely.

GUIDELINES FOR DISTRIBUTING TRACTS

Prayer and Personal Involvement. You should pray about every aspect of your witnessing and look for ways to involve others in a conversation. The tract is no substitute for your personal testimony and witness to others. You can adapt your conversation to the situation at hand while the tract is fixed to a single message. The tract is valuable in many ways, but you should try as well to strike up a conversation. Often asking a question will lead the other person to answer and begin the conversation.

Even when you don't have the chance to speak with the other person, you can pray that the Lord will move him to read the tract. You can pray that the Lord will help him to understand the message. You can pray that God will lead the person to make any decision that needs to be made. As you pray, you recognize the value of the Holy Spirit in your witnessing. As you become personally involved, you carry out your responsibility to evangelize the lost.

Personal Appearance and Manner. It is appropriate to be neatly dressed and to have an attractive manner about you. You should be friendly and confident as you reach out to other people. You represent the Lord and there is no reason to be hesitant or timid in your witness. Be polite.

"Be Prepared." The Boy Scout motto is appropriate when you think of using gospel tracts. You should carry tracts with you wherever and whenever you go. Select tracts that are interesting and appropriate to special situations, and keep them in good condition. Look for opportunities to give them to people you encounter throughout the day. Remember to enclose tracts in your correspondence with businesses or unsaved friends and relatives. Pray that the Lord will use your efforts as you give tracts to others. Be faithful. You may not know the results of your tract distribution until you get to heaven. You may rest assured, however, that the Lord wants you to be faithful to take advantage of the opportunities that come along in your life to give the gospel to others.

CHAPTER SIX

THE PRACTICAL RESOURCES

EVANGELISM INVOLVES A number of practical matters. Some of them are common sense suggestions. Some of them come from my personal experience in past efforts at leading people to trust Jesus Christ. The Bible does not particularly single out these resources, but they are still important matters to keep in mind as you try to win the lost to the Lord. Following these suggestions will make you a better soulwinner. As you practice these steps over and over, they'll become a part of your evangelistic outreach. They will help you win the lost that God brings across your path.

WITNESS TO EVERYONE YOU CAN WITNESS TO

You will meet many unsaved people as you carry out your normal everyday activities. Perhaps you carry on a conversation with your neighbors over the backyard fence. You probably speak several times a day with your coworkers as you carry out your work responsibilities. You may help a friend or neighbor with a home-repair job. You may go shopping and speak with the clerk as you make your purchase. Friends often go out to lunch or dinner together. You may get involved with a variety of other things that come across your path day after day.

God has been working in the hearts of some of the folk whom you meet throughout the day, and they need someone to point them to Jesus Christ. How do you know which ones are struggling with sin? How do you know who is looking for an answer to a question about spiritual matters? How do you know which one has had his heart prepared by the Lord to accept Him as Savior? You don't! But you can rest assured that some of the people you meet need you to witness to them. The only way that you will reach the *some* is by trying to reach the *all*. That means you need to look for opportunities to introduce your witness into the conversation.

You won't reach everyone as you witness, but you will reach some. I spoke to a man in jail about the Lord and got nowhere. A week later, I went to a cell at the opposite end of the jail and found the same man. I witnessed to him and, again, I got nowhere. A week later one of the prison guards sought me out. The man I had witnessed to had been transferred to a jail in North Carolina. A preacher there had visited him and led him to the Lord. He managed to send word back to me of his decision to receive Jesus Christ, along with the comment, "I think Pete would like to know."

One of the students in the Christian school where I served was lost. I called her into my office and tried to lead her to the Lord. She wasn't ready and didn't respond to my efforts to witness to her. A few days later, her piano teacher led her to the Lord. These experiences are not unusual. You won't win everyone to Christ that you witness to. But you don't know which ones whose hearts the Lord has prepared. Only by witnessing to as many as you can of the people who cross your path each day will you reach those who are ready to repent of their sins and accept Jesus Christ as their Savior.

Your responsibility is not to see how many you can lead to pray for forgiveness of sins. Your responsibility is to be faithful. You do what you can do to reach the lost. From time to time, the Lord will work to bring them to Himself. As you witness to others, the Holy Spirit will work in hearts. Some will respond by trusting Christ. Whether you see results or not, you should obey the New Testament commands to tell others of the Lord.

The only way to take advantage of a prepared heart is to reach out to everyone you can as the Lord gives you the opportunity. In addition to winning folks to the Lord as part of my normal ministries, I've had the privilege of leading people to Christ whom I met while walking along the street, while shopping, after picking up a hitchhiker, in my neighborhood, and while carrying on routine responsibilities. I've even led a person to accept the Lord by writing a letter to her. These were not the result of evangelistic ministries but incidental contacts that turned into soulwinning opportunities. You also can reach out to others whom you meet in your daily routine.

Don't Take Salvation for Granted

The fact that someone looks like a Christian and acts like a Christian and talks like a Christian doesn't mean that he is a Christian. You cannot assume that a person knows Jesus Christ as his Savior just because he has a wholesome appearance and seems to have high standards. I remember one of the young men in the Christian school where I was the principal. When I called him in to talk about the Lord, he responded to me by saying, "I'm as good as the rest of the students." That was part of his problem. He was as good as the students he knew. He had been reared in a family in which his parents had set high standards for him. He was polite to others, worked hard as he carried out his responsibilities, did well in his classes, and was well liked by the other students. He was popular enough that his classmates later elected him to a position of responsibility in the school. But he was lost. He trusted Christ only after he found another student whose Christianity he could respect.

I led a young man to the Lord who had grown up in a Christian home and had gone to a fundamental church all his life. He was active in Sunday school, in the young people's meetings at his church on Sunday night, and in prayer meetings. He went to a Christian school, was neat, didn't use profanity, didn't smoke or drink alcoholic beverages, and had never used drugs. He gave every appearance of being a fine young Christian man. He told me, "I always thought I was a Christian because I was in a Christian family." It was only after the Lord brought conviction through a sermon he heard that he realized he needed to make a personal decision to repent of his sins and to receive Jesus Christ as his Savior.

You probably have similar situations among your family, your neighbors, your coworkers, and your friends. You know people who have high personal standards but do not know Jesus Christ as their Savior. They may go regularly to church, but they are not saved. You can't take it for granted that they are Christians just because they look like Christians. My wife and I were having dinner at a local restaurant. As we came in, I noticed another couple seated at a nearby booth. I knew the husband from my work. When they were served, they bowed their heads while the husband returned thanks for the food. I was impressed. I knew the husband professionally and had not thought of him as a Christian. About this time, he noticed me and invited my wife and me to join them. After we had moved to their table, I commented that I had noticed him giving thanks and wondered if he were a Christian. To my surprise, he responded that he was a Mormon. He looked like a Christian but the looks were deceiving. As the old saying goes, "All that glitters is not gold." There's a world of difference between iron pyrite and genuine gold. And the fact that someone looks and acts and talks like a Christian doesn't mean that he is. You need to make sure.

As principal of a Christian school, I called the seniors into my office each year and talked with them about their plans after graduation and also tried to find out something about their relationship to the Lord. One year, there were two boys in the senior class who were both unsaved. I led each of them to the Lord. In both cases, I was surprised. As far as the school was concerned, they were good students. Neither one of them had been in disciplinary trouble at school. Both of them were active in sports, one in basketball and the other in baseball. Their grades were generally good. Both of them went to church regularly. They had been in our school for a couple of years, where they had taken Bible classes and sat through daily chapel messages. But when I asked them why they had not accepted the Lord earlier, both gave me the same answer, "No one ever asked me to before." Their parents, their teachers, their classmates, their Sunday school teachers, the pastors whom they saw regularly at church, and a host of other Christians whom they had rubbed shoulders with had not thought of them as unsaved. They looked and acted like Christians, and everyone assumed they were Christians. But they were lost until I had the opportunity to lead them to accept the Lord. You can't take Christianity for granted.

Be Willing to Put Yourself Out

Lost people are not standing in line waiting to ask me how to be saved. Far from it! In almost every case, the people I have led to profess faith in Jesus Christ as their Savior have been people I encountered because I put myself out in some way. I had to initiate a conversation, to pass out a gospel tract, to drive to a nearby jail or nursing home, to prepare a sermon to preach, or to give up some personal time. Is it worthwhile to make a sacrifice to win someone to Christ? Absolutely! Frankly, it's worthwhile to make a sacrifice for the Lord even if no one comes to Christ. When you think of the sacrifice that Jesus

Christ made for you, it shouldn't be hard to make some trifling sacrifice for Him.

As I passed a corner along a street in San Diego, I looked down the block and saw a sailor standing on the next corner. I thought to myself, if he's still there when I come back, I'm going to witness to him. A few minutes later, as I returned, he was still standing on the corner. I changed directions, walked to him, gave him a tract to read, and started a conversation. No, he wasn't saved. Yes, he was interested in knowing what the Bible had to say. In a few minutes, he bowed his head there on the corner and asked Jesus Christ to forgive his sins and to become his Savior. Was it worthwhile for me to walk an extra two blocks? I don't need to hesitate over that answer. It was worthwhile to walk two blocks, twenty blocks, or two hundred blocks. You will never make a sacrifice too great in your service for the Lord.

Was it worthwhile to drive sixty miles each week—three thousand miles each year—to preach at a jail in return for fifty to sixty decisions for Christ? Was it worthwhile to take the time to give a gas station attendant a tract that led to his decision for the Lord? Was it worthwhile to drive one hundred fifty miles to help put on a fiesta in Mexico that led to several dozen decisions for Christ and the starting of a fundamental Baptist church in that town? Was it worthwhile to take a couple of hours out of my Saturday each week over several years to go on visitation for my church when several people trusted Christ?

You get the idea. You should be willing to make personal sacrifices in order to tell others about the salvation the Lord offers them. As I look back over the years, I can say that in almost every case, I have had to put myself out in some way to bring people to Christ. I can think of only one case in which the unsaved person came to me. I had returned to my office after listening to a chapel speaker. A couple of minutes later, a student came in under conviction from the message and wanted to be saved. He came to me because I was his Bible teacher.

Other than that single student, I have always gone to the unsaved person.

Isn't this what the New Testament teaches? Matthew 28:19 says, "Go ye therefore." Mark 16:15 echoes this by saying, "Go ye into all the world." Acts 1:8 suggests an active role when it says, "Ye shall be witnesses." Nowhere in the Bible are you told to wait until the opportunities come to you. You should put yourself out as you take advantage of the opportunities all around you.

Take Advantage of Opportunities

You can't tell by looking at the people around you which of them have been prepared by the Holy Spirit to receive Jesus Christ. The only way to reach those whose hearts the Lord has prepared is to take advantage of every opportunity that comes along. For most Christians, your local church is an obvious place to start. Most churches are short of people to participate in evangelistic outreaches. Your pastor will be happy to put you to work. He may ask you to teach a Sunday school class, to help in a youth outreach activity, to open your home to host a fellowship group, or to pass out brochures inviting people to some church activity. He may get you involved with visiting folks who have moved into the area or those who have visited the church, counseling people who respond to the invitation, or some other opportunity that is unique to your church. Activity in your local church is good for you and it is good for the church. You will grow spiritually and your church will have its needs for workers met. As you take part in the activities of the church, you put yourself in a position to be able to speak with others about the Lord.

Participating in church visitation is normally open to every church member. If you don't feel comfortable going on visitation, go out with someone who will train you by his or her example. More than forty years ago, I went out with the youth pastor at our church, who showed me what to do at our first visit. He turned the second visit over to me. I was scared stiff that I wouldn't know what to say, but I had the reassurance that he was there to back me up. The visit went fine. Going with an experienced visitor was helpful to me and gave me some needed experience in talking with people about the Lord. Since that time, I've been able to train others in visitation. More importantly, I've had the privilege of leading several people to the Lord whom I've met through the visitation program of my church.

Quite often, your church needs volunteers to work with vacation Bible school. It's a great opportunity, especially for moms who normally stay at home with their children during the year. There is almost always a shortage of workers. VBS activities use many people in many different roles—leading children in singing, telling a missionary or Bible story, doing a flannel graph lesson, working in the nursery to care for the children of the workers, teaching a memory verse, helping with crafts, preparing and serving refreshments, or something else. There is probably something you can do that will add to the program. You may have a support role, but you still have a share in every child who accepts Jesus Christ. My wife and I have used a VBS program as an evangelistic outreach.

If you feel confident of your ability to speak with people who respond to the invitation after a sermon, talk with your pastor about helping with counseling. In large churches, the pastoral staff or the deacons take care of this. Often, however, it is convenient for the pastor to have a woman to call on to speak with a woman who has come forward to have some spiritual need met. Pastors may also wish to have men available to help those who come forward to make decisions about spiritual matters.

Get involved with the soulwinning activities of your church. Some churches hold basketball or game night activities to reach into the community. Some successfully use weightlifting as an outreach to the unsaved. I've been in churches that have distributed gospel literature to every house in the town. Almost every church has an evangelistic meeting once or twice a year, when they pass out literature inviting people to the services. Churches routinely have activities for the teens and children as they try to reach them with the gospel. It's not unusual for a church to have a special soulwinning emphasis in connection with a holiday—the Fourth of July, Veterans' Day, Thanksgiving, Easter, Christmas. Again, someone needs to pass out literature inviting people to these activities. Several fundamental churches may join together to hold a citywide crusade. You can help by singing in the choir, by counseling, by passing out invitations, or in some other way that is unique to your city's situation.

If you own or supervise a business, you should look for ways to use your position to witness to others. I have known business owners who posted signs with Bible verses or placed tracts by the cash register for people to take. I was in an office recently with background music from a Christian radio station and a Bible on the table with the reading material. Many businesses will place signs in their windows advertising an evangelistic meeting or some other church activity. A taxi driver mounted a container of tracts in his back seat with a sign inviting customers to take one. I know an employee who held a Bible study with his employer that resulted in the employer's accepting Christ as his Savior. I know a public school teacher who kept his Bible on his desk. He wasn't permitted to bring up Christianity in the classroom, but he was allowed to answer questions his students asked him. I know of several businessmen who close their businesses on Sunday as part of their testimony. I know of a business owner who held a Bible study with his employees as part of their paid working time. A businessman includes a verse on his business card that refers to the end times. He follows it with the question, "Are you ready to meet the Lord of the Second Coming face to face?" A public school counselor used her position to lead several of her students to the Lord. Every business is different in what it permits and in the opportunities it gives. You may not be able to do what someone else does, but you can find something that fits your situation.

There are also opportunities to witness to people whom you meet during your daily activities. You may be able to speak with the clerk in a store where you've been shopping. You may be able to give a gospel tract to a gas-station or parking-lot attendant. You may invite a neighbor over to your house for refreshments. You may find that your neighbor enjoys fishing or hunting. You may be able to speak with a friend whom you've invited to a ball game. I found that attending a Bible study at the company where I worked let others in my department know that I was a Christian. That gave me the chance to witness. You may be able to talk with a fellow worker as you eat lunch together or even as you work at various jobs. I've found that security guards are often bored and willing to talk. The opportunities are all around you. Ask the Lord to help you see them.

Opportunities sometimes make themselves available for only a short time, then disappear. Be alert for them and take advantage of the chance to witness when it comes up. My wife and I were vacationing in Alaska and had gone a day early to adjust to the time change before we joined a tour group. After a day of sightseeing, I dropped my wife off at the hotel, then took the rental car back to the airport. I called the hotel to ask them to send a courtesy car to pick me up. When the driver arrived, I had about five minutes to talk with him about the Lord before we reached the hotel. After getting in the car, I introduced myself, gave him a tract, found him willing to talk, and so gave the gospel as quickly as I could. When we arrived at the hotel, he bowed his head and asked the Lord to save him. I don't like to rush the presentation of the gospel. I would much rather have some give and take, ask and answer questions, and be sure that the person understands what the Bible says about salvation. But I didn't have that much time. I had to take advantage of the opportunity, then follow up later with a letter to the driver to give him guidance for the Christian life and to recommend a couple of sound churches in the area. You may find a similar situation in which you have to use the time the Lord gives you. Be ready!

You Have the Ability

One of the biggest hindrances to soulwinning is a feeling of inadequacy. You use the excuse that evangelism is for the pastor. You say, I don't know the Bible well enough. You excuse yourself by saying that you don't know what to say. Those excuses don't work! The Bible never tells the pastor to do all the soulwinning in the church. Instead, Paul tells Christian workers that their ministry is "for the perfecting of the saints, for the work of the ministry, for the edifying of the body of Christ" (Eph. 4:12). The Lord gave the command to win the lost to Himself to "the eleven [disciples] . . . and them that were with them" (Luke 24:33). Evangelism is the responsibility of every Christian. Evangelism is your responsibility.

The way to overcome your uncertainty in witnessing is to practice giving the gospel to other people. As you involve yourself in different kinds of soulwinning activities, you will learn how to present the gospel. You will learn what questions people ask and how to answer them. You will gain confidence. You can do it.

I recall taking a senior boy who was in the high school where I taught with me to the jail where I was holding services. After I preached, a man came forward to receive the Lord, so I turned him over to the high school student to lead to the Lord. It was embarrassing. He didn't know what to say. He was tongue-tied. I had to loan him my Bible. I finally had to step back in and talk with the man myself. But some years later, I ran into this same boy, now with a few years of maturity and experience under his belt. This time, however, he was representing a national organization that specialized in evangelism. He had gained experience and was now equipped for the ministry.

A number of years ago, our church had a visitation pastor who spent full time in going door to door to reach the lost. He generally won over two hundred people each year to Christ. I went with him one day to see what his technique was for presenting the gospel. I thought that the experience might help me be a better soulwinner. To my surprise, I found that his technique was much the same as my technique. The reason he won two hundred people each year to the Lord was that he talked with several thousand people. He won more because he witnessed more. You can do the same.

BE PERSISTENT

There is a well-known song that says, "Obedience is the very best way."[1] That is true when it comes to evangelism. The Lord expects you to be obedient to His command to witness to the lost. You won't win everyone you witness to, but you will win some. Don't quit if you go through a time when no one responds to your witness. It is the Lord's responsibility to draw the lost to Himself. It is your responsibility to be faithful, carrying out His command to tell others that Jesus Christ died for them.

Several years ago, I had an unsaved student whom I witnessed to with no response. I called her in to my office to talk with her and found that she was not interested in accepting the Lord. She did, however, say that she was willing to have a short Bible study with me. She would come in and we would go through a portion of the New Testament. We went through Ephesians and Colossians without any positive response from her. She finally told me one day that I had one more chance to talk with her. As I presented the gospel, she suddenly turned away and started to leave. When I stopped her, I could see tears running down her cheeks and realized that she had come under conviction. After talking a few minutes more, she yielded her will to the Lord.

As an administrator at the school, I kept a card file on students I talked with. When a student came in to speak with me, I jotted a sentence or two down summarizing what we had talked about. If a student came in again to see me, a quick look at the card familiarized me with what we had covered before. In this case, when I looked at the card devoted to the girl, I found that she had prayed to receive the Lord on the fiftieth time I had spoken with her about her need of salvation. What if I had given up after ten or twenty times? after thirty or forty times? You do not know when the Holy Spirit will work. Be persistent and don't let discouragement cause you to quit.

Common-Sense Suggestions

There are several practical tips for presenting Christ that will help your witnessing. You should be neat and clean. Avoid bad breath and body odors. Dress in a way that is appropriate. Men should shave or trim their mustaches and beards and comb their hair. I know these things have nothing to do with the gospel, but you represent the Lord. It is right to represent Him to the best of your ability. In a day when slovenly dress and actions are common, you will make a better impression by being neat and clean. You will never offend someone by making a good impression on him, but you may well offend others when you don't.

Be courteous, be tactful, and don't get involved in arguments. I found in preaching at jails that the men would often bring up a question that had nothing to do with the sermon. A favorite question was "Hey preacher, what do you think about capital punishment?" The men didn't really want an answer. They wanted to argue. My standard response was something like, "That's a good question. I'll get back to that as soon as I finish the sermon." I kept to the main point. Normally, the men in jail didn't really care about capital punishment. They wanted to get me off on a rabbit trail. If you get involved in an argument, you may win it because you have the truth of God's Word on your side. If you win the argument, however, you will lose the main point of winning someone to the Lord. Hold that other person to the main point of the need to receive Jesus Christ as Savior. Don't get sidetracked.

In general, deal with persons of your own age and sex. You can't always do this, but when you can, it is easier to speak with folks who have something in common with you. As you speak with others, try to talk with them when there is no one else around to hear the conversation. Many people, probably most people, are embarrassed to talk about spiritual things. They will appreciate your approaching them at a time and in a way that will not cause them to feel self-conscious.

Avoid unnecessary familiarities with those you speak with. Different nationalities communicate in different ways. Some people use their hands and arms in gesturing, some reach out to touch another person, and some hug when they meet another person. You should be careful not to be overly familiar with those you talk to. They may not be used to physical contact with others, and you may hinder your chance of winning them to Christ by being too familiar.

That same principle holds true with your speech. You should be careful not to insult or put down someone. It may offend them.

When the Lord opens the door for you to get involved in a witnessing opportunity, use a minimum number of Scripture verses. Emphasize these truths and explain them clearly. You probably know a great deal more about the Bible than you will use in talking with others. Your purpose is not to impress the other person with how well you know God's Word. Your purpose is to persuade the other person to accept Jesus Christ as Savior. To that end, be simple and clear in your presentation.

If it is convenient, have the other person read out loud the verses that you use. If you read the verses to the other person, he hears them. If he reads them, he both hears and sees them. There is a double impact through the eye and the ear. Be quick to help someone who doesn't read well. You are probably familiar enough with your Bible that you can pronounce the words and understand what it says. Many people, however, do not read well. This is especially true with unfamiliar words and passages in the Bible. Be alert to the times when the other person needs help. As he reads a verse or passage, ask some questions to make sure he understands what the Bible says. When you can, give an illustration to clarify the biblical truth.

When you go on visitation for your church, it is often helpful for two people to go together. I've been on several visits where I would distract a dog while my partner went to the door. I've sat on the floor and played with a child while my partner presented Christ. In our lawsuit-minded society, a second person is a witness that no wrong behavior has taken place. Keep in mind that in the normal case one person should do the talking. You don't know where your partner is going with the conversation. If he is doing the talking, let him lead it while you pray for him.

Remember also that the purpose of a visit for the church is spiritual. I've been on visits when my partner would talk about the weather, about mutual friends, about second or third cousins, about work, about the local ball team, and about a dozen other things. This misses the most important topic of conversation, the gospel of Jesus Christ. I don't mean that you must start with the gospel. It's fine to start out with neutral topics when that's appropriate. But the conversation should move on from there to spiritual matters. When you fail to bring up the spiritual truths of the gospel, you're wasting your time and the time of the other person. Get to what should be the main point of your visit.

As a young man, Simón Bolívar, the liberator of several South American countries, took this oath: "I swear by the God of my forefathers, I swear by my native country, that I shall never give rest to my arm nor to my soul until I have broken the shackles which chain us to Spain!"[2] Would that Christians would have that same determination to break the shackles of sin that bind men to Satan.

CHAPTER SEVEN

THE RESOURCE THAT MOST AVOID

THE MIRACLE OF the healing of the paralyzed man in Mark 2:1–12 is familiar to most Christians. The man could not get to Jesus himself, so four of his friends brought him to the Lord by carrying him on some sort of stretcher. When the friends arrived outside the house where the Lord was teaching, a crowd of people was gathered to listen to Him. The four friends could not get themselves and the stretcher through the throng of people. The friends, however, did not let these circumstances turn them away from their goal. Instead, they climbed to the top of the flat-roofed house. They then pried up several of the tiles that formed the roof and let their friend down through the opening into the room where the Lord was speaking. The faith of the group was obvious. They had gone beyond the call of friendship to get their friend to Jesus. Seeing as well the faith of the sick man, the Lord told him to get up, carry his bed, and return to his home.

There are many questions we could ask about the miracle. How did the four men get their friend up on the roof? How was the tile roof constructed—the tiles were loose enough to be pried up and yet the roof did not leak when it rained? What did the owner of the house and the crowd in the house think about seeing the roof being torn up? Where did the men get the ropes they used to let the stretcher down? These are all legitimate questions, but I want to ask another. Who paid for the roof? The damage had to be repaired. Who paid the bill?

I ask the question because giving is a part of the Christian life. Specifically, it is a part of soulwinning. It is rare that a person comes to Jesus Christ for salvation apart from someone's spending a few dollars. It may be the money that pays the salary of a Christian worker who preaches and teaches the Bible. It may be money spent to build a church where the gospel message will go forth week by week. It may be pooling your money with that of other Christians in order to send a missionary to some foreign country. It may only be paying for gasoline in the car as you go on visitation. It may be purchasing some gospel tracts that you will give out to others. It may be buying some new materials for a Sunday school class you teach or for a vacation Bible school activity. It may be money spent for the cost of refreshments at a youth group meeting at your house. I could go on but this should make the idea clear. Christians must give their money in order that lost souls can be saved. As William Grimshaw, a mid-eighteenth-century preacher in Great Britain, said, "Do good in the world with the goods of this world."[1] The good that you're after is the good of seeing souls come to Jesus Christ for salvation.

The Bible clearly teaches the principle of giving. When you give, you show your faith in the Lord. "Zacchaeus stood, and said unto the Lord; Behold, Lord, the half of my goods I give to the poor; and if I have taken any thing from any man by false accusation, I restore him fourfold" (Luke 19:8). George Goodman, an early twentieth-century Bible teacher and preacher, well said, "A personal religion is a purse-and-all religion."[2] Your willingness to give money for the support of God's work shows your belief that His way is best.

Giving is also a mark of your righteousness: "As it is written, He hath dispersed abroad; he hath given to the poor: his righteousness remaineth for ever" (II Cor. 9:9). Samuel Robbins Brown, a nineteenth-century pioneer missionary to Japan, said, "Large-hearted people are the happiest, because they are most like God."[3]

Failing to give makes your Christianity hypocritical. "[If] one of you say unto [a poor person], Depart in peace, be ye warmed and filled; notwithstanding ye give them not those things which are needful to the body; what doth it profit?" (James 2:16). In order to show that you have a genuine concern for others, you must be willing to give what you can to meet their needs. Your giving for the purposes of soulwinning shows that you are sincere in your desire to see the lost come to Jesus Christ.

God gave to bring eternal life to you: "For God so loved the world, that he gave his only begotten Son, that whosoever believeth in him should not perish, but have everlasting life" (John 3:16). "He that spared not his own Son, but delivered him up for us all, how shall he not with him also freely give us all things?" (Rom. 8:32). "And this is the record, that God hath given to us eternal life, and this life is in his Son" (I John 5:11). If God gave sacrificially to you, shouldn't you be willing to give sacrificially to Him? Whatever you give to the Lord's work, it is far less than He gave for you.

The Lord has given you eternal life, He has also given you spiritual gifts that you may use in your service to Him. "Having then gifts differing according to the grace that is given to us" (Rom. 12:6). "As every man hath received the gift, even so minister the same one to another, as good stewards of the manifold grace of God" (I Pet. 4:10). In the light of this, doesn't it seem reasonable that you should give from what you have to bring eternal life to others?

Since giving shows your faithfulness to God, He has promised to reward those who give to further His work: "But this

I say, He which soweth sparingly shall reap also sparingly; and he which soweth bountifully shall reap also bountifully. Every man according as he purposeth in his heart, so let him give; not grudgingly, or of necessity: for God loveth a cheerful giver" (II Cor. 9:6–7). God not only rewards those who give, He rewards them abundantly: "Give, and it shall be given unto you; good measure, pressed down, and shaken together, and running over, shall men give into your bosom. For with the same measure that ye mete withal it shall be measured to you again" (Luke 6:38).

Several years ago I was riding with a friend in his car to the garage he owned, where I planned to pick up my own car. As we drove, we talked about giving to the church. He commented, "Pastor said that if we'd tithe, God would bless us. I tithed for a week, but my business didn't pick up, so I quit." He had missed the whole point of God's blessing. God may bless you financially, but there are a thousand other areas in which he may bless you as well. He may bless your health, your family, your plans for the future, your relationship with Him, your business, your friendships, and many other areas as well. God rewards those who give, not with salvation—that comes by faith in Christ's sacrifice alone—but with blessing in this world and in the world to come.

It's not the amount of money you give that God looks at. Some of you can write checks for thousands of dollars and never miss the money. Many of us have to be careful when we write a check for a few dollars. The Lord illustrated this to His disciples:

> And Jesus sat over against the treasury, and beheld how the people cast money into the treasury: and many that were rich cast in much. And there came a certain poor widow, and she threw in two mites, which make a farthing. And he called unto him his disciples, and saith unto them, Verily I say unto you, That this poor widow hath cast more in, than all they which have cast into the treasury: for all they did cast in of their

abundance; but she of her want did cast in all that she had, even all her living. (Mark 12:41–44)

The Lord made it clear that He rewards the act of giving, no matter how little may be involved. "Whosoever shall give to drink unto one of these little ones a cup of cold water only in the name of a disciple, verily I say unto you, he shall in no wise lose his reward" (Matt. 10:42). The Lord follows this principle because He looks at the attitude of your heart as you give, not at the amount you give. "For if there be first a willing mind, it is accepted according to that a man hath, and not according to that he hath not" (II Cor. 8:12). James B. Chapman, early twentieth-century preacher, evangelist, educator, author, and editor, said, "It is not how much you give, but how much you have left that measures your devotion to Christ."[4]

The final rewards will not take place in this life. The Lord will give them to His faithful followers in the life to come: "Behold, I come quickly; and my reward is with me, to give every man according as his work shall be" (Rev. 22:12). "For the Son of man shall come in the glory of his Father with his angels; and then he shall reward every man according to his works" (Matt. 16:27). Your giving now lays up treasure in heaven for the life to come.

Many religious groups are competing for your money. Be careful that you support only ministries that are faithful to the Word of God. The First Church of What's Happening Now may have a wonderful social program to relieve the burdens of unfortunates. I wouldn't give them a dime if they didn't work evangelism into their social activities. It is unfortunate that many Christians give to support the work of the Devil. Let's face it. Satan is smarter than the average Christian is. He knows that a clever name, an attractively described social work, some color pictures, and perhaps a slick-talking representative can work together to take large amounts of money away from true Christian ministries.

Giving money away goes contrary to human nature. But the Bible teaches that "the love of money is the root of all [kinds of] evil" (I Tim. 6:10). The book of Acts illustrates this: "[Felix] hoped also that money should have been given him of Paul, that he might loose him: wherefore he sent for him the oftener, and communed with him" (Acts 24:26). We see the sad example of greed in Ananias and Sapphira (Acts 5:1–11). Both paid a heavy penalty for falsely trying to impress others with what they had given. Perhaps the classic example of greed comes from Judas Iscariot, who having finally realized that Jesus Christ was not going to set up an earthly kingdom, and that he would not have a place of prominence in it, went to the priests to arrange the betrayal of the Lord. "Judas Iscariot, one of the twelve, went unto the chief priests, to betray him unto them. And when they heard it, they were glad, and promised to give him money. And he sought how he might conveniently betray him" (Mark 14:10–11). For thirty pieces of silver, he sold his soul to the Devil.

The New Testament gives you some guidelines for your giving. You should trust in God, not in your money: "Charge them that are rich in this world, that they be not highminded, nor trust in uncertain riches, but in the living God, who giveth us richly all things to enjoy" (I Tim. 6:17). I know it's easier to trust in something you can see than to trust in someone whom you can't see. Once again, that's human nature, and your Christianity should not give in to that temptation.

Rather than greed, the Lord wants you to be content with what He provides: "But godliness with contentment is great gain. For we brought nothing into this world, and it is certain we can carry nothing out. And having food and raiment let us be therewith content" (I Tim. 6:6–8). There's a familiar saying that aptly describes the believer's situation: "There's nothing wrong with living a hand-to-mouth existence, as long as it's God's hand giving food for your mouth."

Your giving should be in proportion to your income: "Upon the first day of the week let every one of you lay by him in store, as God hath prospered him, that there be no gatherings when I come" (I Cor. 16:2). Did you get that? Your giving should be "as God hath prospered [you]." That verse also teaches that your giving should be regular, "upon the first day of the week," when you come together at church to worship with other believers. The standard of "tithes and offerings" (Mal. 3:8) still sets a worthy practice for Christians to follow.

Yet another principle of giving is that you should earn your income and give from what you have earned. "Let him that stole steal no more: but rather let him labour, working with his hands the thing which is good, that he may have to give to him that needeth" (Eph. 4:28). There is nothing wrong with receiving a gift of money or property of some value. There is nothing wrong with receiving an inheritance. That's not what I'm talking about. God is not looking for lazy Christians to serve Him. He wants hard-working and dependable believers. You prove that you are faithful and reliable by working at a job and then by giving to the Lord from your income.

Putting the above all together, it is clear that the New Testament teaches that believers should give. Despite this teaching, most Christians give only a small amount to Christian ministries. One Barna poll found that only 3 percent of people tithed their income in 2002. Following the terrorist plane crashes on September 11, 2001, and the accounting scandals in several national businesses, 2002 was a bad year economically for the United States, and the percent of giving went down. But in the previous year, the percent who tithed was only 8 percent, still a small amount. When the poll surveyed "evangelicals," the percentage leaped to a not-so-whopping 9 percent in 2002.[5] Most Christians do not follow the biblical teaching in this area.

You will sometimes hear people say something similar to "I don't like that church. They're always talking about money."

Comments like that reveal several things. In the first place, it is rare that a church is always talking about money. I'm not talking about television *escam*gelists. I'm talking about the average pastor in the average church. He may preach on giving from time to time, just as he preaches on salvation, dedication, prayer, love, faithfulness, the need to serve, and a hundred other topics regularly. He preaches on giving because giving is part of the Christian life. It's a biblical command.

In the second place, people who make comments like that would probably find something else to criticize if they didn't talk about money. The unsaved person and the carnal Christian often criticize biblical preaching. If they didn't criticize it, they would have to face their anemic spiritual conditions honestly. Those who criticize the pastor for mentioning the need to give are usually the same ones who give very little or nothing to God's work. George Grenfell, a pioneer missionary to Africa, was accurate with his comment "How seldom do we hear a hundred [dollar check] say, 'I was glad when they said unto me, let us go up to the house of the Lord.'"[6]

Finally, folks who are dedicated to the Lord don't find it hard to give. They give because they love the Lord. They give, often sacrificially, and they wish they had more to give. I was in a church once that was beginning a building program. We didn't want to borrow the money—we believed that paying interest was a waste of the Lord's money—so the pastor challenged the people to double-tithe for one year while the building was going up. Many of us accepted the challenge and gave double or more to the church than we would usually give. Others who had never tithed began to tithe for the first time. What a thrill it was to see the new auditorium completely paid for. It was even a greater thrill to find that we had not only paid off the building but had been able to give more to missions that year than we had given to the building program. We met a need at home without sacrificing the needs on the foreign field. We found out what John Henry Jowett, an early twentieth-century pastor in both the United States and Great Britain, expressed: "We begin to operate with vital forces when we cross the border into the land of sacrifices. The things that we can spare carry no sacrifice blood. The things that we cannot spare carry part of ourselves and are alive."[7]

You can't expect the Lord to be pleased with your money until you have first given yourself to Him. He wants total dedication from you. "And this [the churches of Macedonia] did, not as we hoped, but first gave their own selves to the Lord, and unto us by the will of God" (II Cor. 8:5). "I beseech you therefore, brethren, by the mercies of God, that ye present your bodies a living sacrifice, holy, acceptable unto God, which is your reasonable service" (Rom. 12:1). By joining your personal dedication to the Lord with your gifts to His work on earth, you can expect spiritual fruit as the result.

In many cases, the Lord will give you the privilege of seeing fruit from your gifts. Once when I was preaching at a small work, my wife and I put on a vacation Bible school for the children. We bought the visualized songs, a missionary story, and the refreshments. We paid for the flyers advertising the special week. We averaged about ten children each evening when we met. And one of the girls prayed to receive the Lord. Did that make our time and expense worthwhile? There's no question about it. It was worth all that we put into the week.

That can be repeated many times over. You may lead someone to Christ using some gospel tracts that you've purchased. You may see someone walk down the aisle to confess Jesus Christ as his or her Savior at the church you support. You may invite a friend or coworker out for a cup of coffee and see him pray to receive the Lord. God often gives you the privilege of seeing the fruit from your giving.

Sometimes, however, your giving requires faith that God will bless the gift. You may never see the results that come from your gift. I've given to the support of missions for years and have never seen the first convert. I've heard missionaries tell about converts, and I'm satisfied that God has blessed my gifts. But I've never seen the converts with my own eyes. That's not unusual. You may see some photos of converts on a field, but unless you visit the field, you won't see them for yourself. Unless you learn the language, you won't speak with them yourself. You give with faith that God will bless your gifts.

You may give to support an activity that does not bring forth any visible result. You may purchase tracts to give away that do not give you an immediate result. Many times, the money that you give just sows the gospel seed. It may bring forth its result months or years later, when you're not around to see it.

Whether God gives you the privilege of seeing a result or not, it is still right to give. Your gifts are absolutely necessary to help soulwinning efforts go forward. You help them go forward at home and you help them go forward on foreign fields. You give and you pray that God will bless your gifts. And you leave the results to Him. He will do His work in the hearts of the lost. You'll have all eternity to speak with those you have helped come to Christ.

CHAPTER EIGHT

THE TRADITIONAL RESOURCE (AND OTHERS)

BEGINNING THE CONVERSATION

MANY CHRISTIANS USE the difficulty of beginning a conversation as an excuse to keep from speaking with others about the Lord. They say they don't know what to say or they don't know how to bring up spiritual matters. You can talk with complete strangers about the weather, about politics, about local or professional sports, about the recent news, about a local school or college, about any of a dozen or more topics, but you don't know how to bring up the matters that relate to salvation. You've seen it happen in your own experience. You are in a line waiting to pay for your groceries. You turn to someone you have never met and bring up some meaningless topic without any hesitation. But you don't bring up spiritual things. Instead, you keep quiet about the most important topic of all.

Now, I agree that you should be tactful. You should not embarrass other people. You should not insult them. You should recognize that you're intruding into their privacy, and, if they don't want to talk about the Lord, that is their right. You can't force them to discuss Christianity. You can, however, offer them the opportunity. If they respond, you can move into a conversation about spiritual things. Quite often, in speaking with people, they will mention something that you can relate to your church. Perhaps they'll mention sports, and you can tell them about a sports activity that your church has sponsored, a sports banquet, a game your Christian school recently played, or a Christian speaker who played professional sports. They may mention a job and you can respond, "Oh yes, I have a friend at church who works there" or "I have a man in my Sunday school class who does that for a living." They may mention some school and you can tell them of someone in your church who attends (or attended) that school. They may mention a name of someone who is a relative of someone in your church. The point is that you can often use some secular matter to make a transition to your church. From there, you move into a conversation designed to bring them to Christ.

While I was flying to San Diego for a vacation, I was seated next to a lady who lived there. When she told me the section of town she lived in, I said, "I've been to your house." It was thirty years before, when I was working as a door-to-door salesman while I was still in college. I'd been to every house in that area of town. Bringing up that part of town gave us something in common that we could talk about. Then I asked if she attended church anywhere in that area. That's what I call a "religiously neutral question." It quite often will lead into a more directly spiritual conversation. From there, I could present the gospel to her. She didn't respond, but she heard the truth she needed to hear.

My wife and I were flying to Montana a couple of years ago for vacation. The airline hadn't been able to seat us together, so I was in a seat with another man who was flying to the same destination. It was a simple matter to find out where he was going and if he went to church anywhere, and then to present the gospel. Again, he didn't respond, but he heard the message that Jesus Christ could save him.

Once you have made the transition to spiritual subjects, there are many probing questions that will tell whether someone is a Christian. Probably the question I most often ask is "If you were to die today, do you know that you would go to heaven?" You can vary the question: "Do you know that you are going to heaven?" or "If the Lord were to ask you why He should let you into heaven, what would you say?" or "Has anyone ever showed you from the Bible how to be saved?" or something similar. The response the person gives you will often give you an idea of whether he knows the Lord as his Savior.

If a person responds and seems willing to discuss spiritual things, you should move into what the Bible has to say about the steps that will lead him to salvation. You should always have a Bible or a New Testament with you. Women can easily slip one into their purse or into a pocket. Most men can carry a New Testament in their hip pocket or in the inside pocket of a suit coat. You may carry it with you for years and not need it, but when the need arises, you want to have it available. By carrying it with you every day, you let the Lord know that you want to carry out His last command to win others to Him. You also prepare yourself to witness when the opportunity comes along.

THE PLAN OF SALVATION

Christians often call the steps that lead a person to salvation the "plan of salvation." This includes a series of logical steps that take a person from seeing his problem of sin and its punishment to understanding the solution that Jesus Christ offers. There are several approaches that soulwinners use.

The Romans Road. The most common approach used by soulwinners has the name "The Romans Road." It has acquired this name because all the verses used with the various steps come from the book of Romans.

1. Begin with *the fact of sin.* "For all have sinned, and come short of the glory of God" (Rom. 3:23). I usually point out that this does not mean that they have committed every sin that it's possible to commit. Some people are generally moral and some people are generally immoral. It makes no difference—all are sinners. A single sin makes a person a sinner. Nearly every person will agree that he has sinned. In the almost fifty years I have spoken with people about Christianity, I've had only one person who said that he'd never sinned. He had been brainwashed by the Black Muslims. Even though he was in jail charged with two counts of murder, assault with a deadly weapon, and several other related charges, he didn't think he was a sinner. He thought whites had oppressed blacks for so many years that he was only taking back what was rightfully his. That's extreme! Most people know they have sinned.

2. This leads naturally to *the penalty for sin.* "For the wages of sin is death; but the gift of God is eternal life through Jesus Christ our Lord" (Rom. 6:23). Nearly everyone knows what wages are, but just in case they don't, it's worthwhile explaining it. Usually, a simple question will do the job: "Do you know what wages are?" Or you can illustrate: "When you work, do you expect your employer to pay you?" The wages of sin let a person earn the penalty of death. The wages of sin have never changed. They are the same today that they were in biblical times. People still earn death by their sins.

3. Just to be sure we're talking about the same thing, I often insert a point to make it clear that there is a *physical death* and a *spiritual death.* "So then every one of us shall give account of himself to God" (Rom. 14:12). While the context of this verse relates directly to Christians judging

one another, it makes the clear point that all will stand before God in judgment. The sinner needs to know that God will one day judge his actions. After his physical death will come his spiritual death. The Lord will give him exactly what he has earned with his life.

4. Very clearly, there is a problem. All have sinned, and all will face God in judgment. There is no human way of escape. But God, in His grace, has provided a way to escape His judgment: There is *provision for* sin. Christ has paid the penalty for sin: "For when we were yet without strength, in due time Christ died for the ungodly. . . . But God commendeth his love toward us, in that, while we were yet sinners, Christ died for us" (Rom. 5:6, 8). The infinitely righteous God-man died for the infinite penalty of all the sins of mankind for all time. God gave His only begotten Son as the provision for man's sin.

5. I often insert a point here that can be left out if time is a problem. Many people have the idea that, at death, God will total up the good in their life and weigh it against the bad. If they are *gooder* than they are *badder*, they'll go into heaven. Hell, then, is only for the really bad people. That's not what the Bible teaches. For that reason, I will normally point out that a sinner *cannot earn his salvation by good works*: "But to him that worketh not, but believeth on him that justifieth the ungodly, his faith is counted for righteousness" (Rom. 4:5). If a person can work his way into heaven, there would have been no need for the death of Christ. That person could strut around heaven throughout eternity saying, "I made it on my own. I didn't need the blood of Christ to get me here." So I try to stress that good works do not give a person the right to enter heaven. A person with good works is still a sinner. He may be a pretty good person, but he's still a sinner, and he still needs salvation. The Romans Road does not make the sinner pay a toll. It is

the freely given pathway to heaven. Jesus Christ has paid the price already. The sinner cannot do anything that will add value to the sacrifice of Christ at Calvary.

6. This brings me to the final step. In order to be saved, the sinner *must accept Jesus Christ* as his Savior: "That if thou shalt confess with thy mouth the Lord Jesus, and shalt believe in thine heart that God hath raised him from the dead, thou shalt be saved. For with the heart man believeth unto righteousness; and with the mouth confession is made unto salvation. For whosoever shall call upon the name of the Lord shall be saved" (Rom. 10:9–10, 13). I take the time to explain this.

   a. The sinner must *believe* that Jesus Christ died for him. The Lord's death at Calvary is the only thing that God will ever require. The death of Jesus Christ paid the penalty the sinner deserves. By believing this, you turn from your own good works and rely totally on the work Jesus Christ did for you. Verse 9 specifically mentions belief in the Resurrection. This is the miracle that crowned the work of Christ. As long as the Lord remained in the grave, there was no reason to believe that His death differed from the death of anyone else. It was the Resurrection that showed that God the Father had accepted the sacrifice offered by God the Son. The New Testament stresses the resurrection of Christ (cf. Acts 1:22; 2:24, 30–32; 4:2, 10, 33; Romans 1:4; 4:24, 25).

   I usually stress that "belief" here is more "trust" or "faith" than simple belief. I believe that my car will start when I turn the ignition switch, but I do not trust that for my salvation. There is a difference between intellectual belief and faith. I often illustrate it by recalling the time the doctor told me that there was one of three things wrong with me. I either had cancer or a tumor or a simple infection. It was probably the last, but the only way he could find out was by going inside me to check. When I went onto the operating table, I had more than mere intellectual belief in my doctor. I literally put my life into his hands. (By the way, it was the infection and was easy to treat!) That's what you do when you accept Jesus Christ as your Savior. You rest your eternal destiny on the fact that Jesus died for you.

b. The belief should be strong enough that the sinner will *talk* about it. We readily talk about things that are important to us. I have no hesitation in saying that I love my wife. I don't mind saying that I like to watch baseball on TV. I'll talk with strangers about my flower garden. In the same way, I don't mind telling others that I have trusted Jesus Christ for my salvation. A strong belief should lead to telling others about it.

c. The sinner should *ask* the Lord to save him. God promises that those who "shall call upon the name of the Lord shall be saved." By praying, the sinner shows his faith that God means what He has said.

After explaining these things, I ask the person if he is ready to ask the Lord to save him. Quite often, he will say something like, "What do I say?" I would prefer that he tell the Lord what he wants, so I encourage him to simply talk to the Lord as he would another person. "Tell the Lord that you've sinned, that you believe that Jesus Christ died for you, and that you want Him to forgive your sin and to help you live for Him." I ask him to pray out loud. I like to hear his prayer to be sure he understands what he's doing. I also pray out loud after him, asking God's blessing and guidance for him.

Occasionally, a person will be so embarrassed that he can't pray. That's not surprising. Many people haven't been to church since they were children, and they simply don't know how to pray. I will then pray out loud for the person, asking him to repeat what I say after me as long as he agrees with what I'm saying. His prayer is his way of asking the Lord to save him.

When a person comes to Christ for salvation, he should at the same time have the desire to stop his sin. Paul touches on this in Romans: "Or despisest thou the riches of his goodness and forbearance and longsuffering; not knowing that the goodness of God leadeth thee to repentance?" (Rom. 2:4). Giving up his sins does not save a person, but he should understand that habits of sin should not mark Christians. If he comes to Christ to gain forgiveness for his sins, it doesn't make sense for him to continue in those same sins. You should take the time to explain repentance for sin and the need to build godly habits of living into a life. He probably won't change overnight, but over a period of time, he can learn that habits of righteousness will give him a much more satisfactory life. With time, he can build those godly habits into his life.

It may help you to make a "road map" in your Bible or New Testament. All you have to remember is Romans 3:23. At the bottom of that page, write 6:23. At the bottom of the page where you find 6:23, write 14:12. At the bottom of the page where you find 14:12, write 5:6, 8. At the bottom of the page where you find 5:6, 8, write 4:5. And at the bottom of the page where you find 4:5, write 10:9–10, 13. This will help you remember the points in order as you witness to others about the Lord.

The Ephesians Road (or *The Ephesians Expressway*). Several years ago, when I was going regularly to jail to speak to folks about the Lord, I would often have the opportunity to preach to a tank of men. At other times, I would do personal work with men or women in the individual cells. I never knew whether I would preach until I came to the jail and saw how many others were there that day to work with the prisoners. I needed a sermon I could preach at any time. In searching for a text, I stumbled across Ephesians 2:1–10. It was perfect since it gave me the major points of the plan of salvation in a logical order.

1. *The Fact of Sin.* "And you hath he quickened, who were dead in trespasses and sins" (Eph. 2:1). From this, I made the point that all men are spiritually dead because of their sins.

2. *The Penalty for Sin.* "And were by nature the children of wrath" (Eph. 2:3). Because of their sin, they become members of the group that deserve God's wrath, everlasting punishment in hell.

3. *The Provision for Sin.* "But God, who is rich in mercy, for his great love wherewith he loved us, even when we were dead in sins, hath quickened us together with Christ, (by grace ye are saved)" (Eph. 2:4–5). While God hates the sin and must punish those who are guilty of sin, God loves mankind and has graciously given His Son to pay the penalty they deserve to pay.

4. *Receiving the Gift.* "For by grace are ye saved through faith; and that not of yourselves: it is the gift of God: not of works, lest any man should boast" (Eph. 2:8–9). Sinners receive God's gift by placing their faith in what Christ has done. They cannot do good works to earn salvation since that would let them boast over what they had done. They must put their faith in Jesus Christ.

5. *Living the Christian Life.* This is not a part of the plan of salvation, but it fits so logically that I may add it when I use this passage to speak with someone about Christ. A person is saved to do "good works" (Eph. 2:10). When he repents of his sins, he needs to replace them with godly works. This is God's will for Christians.

There are a couple of advantages to the Ephesians Road. It gives a passage that can be preached without preparation. I add illustrations in the sermon at appropriate places to clarify the points as I make them. The second advantage is that I don't have to flip around from page to page as I look for a verse to support the next point I want to make. I have the plan of salvation in one place, and I don't have to interrupt my witness by turning pages to find the next verse.

As with the Romans Road, you can also mark the points in your Bible or Testament. In this case, since all the points will be on one or two pages, the plan is simpler. Just put a small "1" by the phrase "trespasses and sins." Write a small "2" by the phrase "children of wrath." Add a small "3" by the phrase "quickened together with Christ." Mark a small "4" by verses 8 and 9. Finish with a small "5" by the phrase "good works."

The Titus Road (or *The Titus Trail*). Since I visited jail every week, I faced the same situation over and over. There was a good possibility that I would preach to the same men two or three weeks in a row. Because of this, I looked for another passage that would give me the plan of salvation without the need to go from place to place. I found my next passage in Titus 3:3–6.

1. *The Fact of Sin.* "For we ourselves also were sometimes foolish, disobedient, deceived, serving divers lusts and pleasures, living in malice and envy, hateful, and hating one another" (Titus 3:3). You can see this as you look at the world around you. Unfortunately, you can also see this when you look at yourself—before coming to Christ for salvation. The verse is an up-to-date commentary on life today.

2. *The Punishment of Sin.* Since there is not a clear reference to punishment in this passage, I explain this in connection with verse 3. Since man has sinned, God will punish him. Most people don't have any difficulty seeing this. They punish their children when they break a rule of the family. The state punishes its citizens when they break laws. In the same way, God punishes those who break His laws.

3. *The Provision for Sin.* I next move on to talk about God's provision for the sins of mankind. God loves the sinner and has made a way for him to escape this punishment: "But after that the kindness and love of God our Saviour toward man appeared" (Titus 3:4). Jesus Christ came into this world to die for sinners. His appearance in the world demonstrated the love of God for mankind.

4. *The Free Gift of Salvation.* "Not by works of righteousness which we have done, but according to his mercy he saved us" (Titus 3:5). The Lord has done it all. There is nothing left for sinners to do.

5. *Receiving the Gift.* "Which he shed on us abundantly through Jesus Christ our Saviour" (Titus 3:6). Notice the pronouns "us" and "our." The sinner must receive Jesus Christ as his or her Savior in order to make salvation personal. At this point, you would explain the need to repent of sins—it doesn't make sense to ask the Lord to forgive your sins while planning to keep doing them. You would also explain the need to pray as the sinner asks the Lord to forgive his sins and to save him.

If I am doing personal work, I may skip verse 8. If, however, I use the passage as a text for a sermon, I will usually include verse 8 as a fifth point, the need for a Christian to do good works. I think that sinners should know that the Lord places responsibilities on Christians. Getting saved does not mean that you can continue to live the same kind of life as in the past. There should be a change, and verse 8 lets me make that emphasis.

This passage has the same advantages as Ephesians 2:1–10. Titus 3:3–6 is a passage that I can preach without preparation, and it is a passage I can use to present the main points of the plan of salvation. As before, you can easily mark the phrases to remind you of the points you want to make.

John's Road (or *John's Journey*). I found one more passage for the same purpose. In this case, I chose John 3 and picked several verses out of the chapter to make my points. I have to skip around a bit, but all the verses are in the same chapter, close enough that it is not a problem to find the right page.

1. *The Fact of Sin.* "And this is the condemnation, that light is come into the world, and men loved darkness rather than light, because their deeds were evil. For every one that doeth evil hateth the light, neither cometh to the light, lest his deeds should be reproved" (John 3:19–20). This is one of the clearest verses in the New Testament relating to sin. Wicked men love darkness, they have evil deeds, and they hate the light that came into the world through Jesus Christ.

2. *The Penalty for Sin.* "He that believeth on him is not condemned: but he that believeth not is condemned already, because he hath not believed in the name of the only begotten Son of God. . . . He that believeth not the Son shall not see life; but the wrath of God abideth on him" (John 3:18, 36*b*). Sinful man clearly awaits the judgment of God.

3. *The Provision for Sin.* "For God so loved the world, that he gave his only begotten Son, that whosoever believeth in him should not perish, but have everlasting life" (John 3:16). Charles Wesley's hymn aptly captures this thought: "Amazing love! How can it be, That Thou, my God, shouldst die for me?"

4. *The Need to Believe.* "Whosoever believeth in him should not perish, but have everlasting life. . . . He that believeth on him is not condemned. . . . He that believeth on the Son hath everlasting life" (John 3:16*b*, 18*a*, 36*a*). As before, this is a strong belief, a confident trust that the atoning death of Jesus Christ is the only thing God will ever require for the salvation of the sinner.

Isaiah's Road (or *Isaiah's Interstate*). We can find these same truths in the Old Testament. While this might not be the best approach for most witnessing efforts, the Old Testament is appropriate if you have the opportunity to present the gospel to a Jewish person. I have used Isaiah 52:13–53:12 to present Christ when witnessing to a Jewish friend. It's not as complete as one of the New Testament passages, but it still lets you describe the atoning work of the Lord.

1. *The Fact of Sin.* Verse 5 refers to "our transgressions" and "our iniquities." Verse 6 mentions "the iniquity of us all." Verse 8 speaks of "the transgression of my people." Verse 10 mentions "sin." Verse 11 refers to "iniquities." Using a highlighter on these phrases makes it simple to point them out.

2. *The Punishment for Sin.* The passage in Isaiah does not mention any punishment for sin. It is, however, logical that a person who has sinned should receive some punishment for what he has done. Most people with whom you speak will readily recognize that God will one day judge them for their sins.

3. *The Provision for Sin.* The passage in Isaiah is very clear on this point. In the opening chapter, verse 15 says that He will "sprinkle many nations." The word translated "sprinkle" occurs two dozen times in the Old Testament. It often refers to the sprinkling of blood on the altar during a sacrifice. The sprinkling of an animal's blood on the altar showed the offering of the animal as a substitutionary sacrifice.

In addition, chapter 53 refers several times to the sacrifice of the Lord for sin. Verse 4 states that He was "smitten of God, and afflicted." Verse 5 explains this: "He was wounded [better 'pierced' as in the nails driven through the Lord's hands and feet and the sword piercing His side] for our transgressions." He "was bruised [or 'crushed,' referring to the emotional burden carried by the Lord as He bore man's sins] for our iniquities." In addition, "the chastisement of our peace was upon him" as He suffered chastening in order to bring about peace with God for sinful man.

Verse 6 is the classic verse in the passage that deals with God's provision for our sins. Our sins have caused us, like sheep, to stray from God's ways. This thought became clearer to me when I was driving north through Utah one summer. We had to stop while some sheep were being moved from one pasture to another. Three men and a dog had their hands (and paws) full as they tried to keep the sheep together. The sheep wanted to wander everywhere along the road except in the right direction. Like them, we have gone our own ways. The Lord, however, has laid on Jesus Christ "the iniquity of us all."

4. *Accepting the Sacrifice.* As with the *Punishment for Sin*, the chapter does not mention the need to accept the sacrificial death of the Lord. It is logical, though, that a sacrifice is effective only if it is your sacrifice. The phrase in verse 11, "by his knowledge shall my righteous servant justify many," suggests that not all are justified. This comes only to the "many" who accept the sacrificial death of the Lord as their sacrifice.

The winning of a soul to Christ is important enough that you should have some approach memorized or marked in your Bible. It really doesn't make much difference which approach you follow. The *Romans Road*, the *Ephesians Road*, the *Titus Road, John's Road,* and *Isaiah's Road* all end at the same point. The lost person needs to confess his sin and to ask the Lord to become his Savior. Your responsibility is to take him through these steps so that he understands that he has a sin problem and that there is a solution to the problem. Try the different approaches at different witnessing opportunities, and find the one that you feel most comfortable with. Not everyone will respond to your witness. You can't do anything about that. The response is the Lord's business. It is the Holy Spirit Who draws men and women to the Lord. Your responsibility is to carry out the Lord's last command as you give lost people the opportunity to be saved.

Let me suggest a couple of steps that may help you. You need to learn one of these approaches. Memorize the steps and, at least, the reference to the verses that supports those steps. It is better if you can memorize the verse itself. There will be times when it is not convenient to use your Bible or New Testament. It is helpful if you can simply quote the verse to the other person.

Next, get alone in a room and pretend that you are witnessing to someone. Go through the plan of salvation several times so that you know the points well. Then, sit down with a friend and talk your way through the points that lead to salvation as though you were leading him to the Lord. Have him play the role of a lost person. Perhaps you can turn it around and have him try to lead you to accept the Lord. If necessary, do this two or three times until you feel confident about what you are going to say.

For those of you who are married, try carrying out one or more of these approaches with your spouse. It's worthwhile for a married couple to give some mutual emphasis to the Lord. If you're embarrassed, try it anyway. The one who loves you is going to make it as easy as possible for you to be successful in your soulwinning activities. After going through the steps several times, you'll find your confidence growing.

Finally, go on church visitation with someone who has some experience. Ask your pastor or youth pastor if you can go with him on visitation. Observe his technique. Have him observe your technique, and invite him to make suggestions. That may be embarrassing, but it's better to suffer some temporary discomfort than to make mistakes. Once your pastor knows of your zeal in this area, he may ask you to deal with people who come forward at the invitation for salvation.

If your Christianity is worth having—and it is—then it is worth sharing with those you come into contact with. These may include your family members, neighbors, friends, coworkers, or others you meet casually throughout the day. Having a plan that gives the steps to salvation will increase your confidence as you set out to tell others about the salvation that God offers them through Jesus Christ.

CHAPTER NINE

THE RESOURCE THAT WILL SOON BE GONE

THERE IS ONE more important resource that God has given to Christians. He doesn't give you the same amount that he gives to someone else. Not everyone can use this resource in the same way. Whether you use the resource or not, you will soon find that it is completely gone with no chance of recovering it. The resource is time, time in which you can make contacts with the lost, work at building these contacts into friendly relationships, turn the friendships to spiritual things, and lead others to accept Jesus Christ as their Savior.

A freelance contractor friend of mine met another man in the same business. Over several months, they met occasionally for lunch or on some connection with a job. It was natural to speak with this friend about the Lord, about the Bible, or about church. It didn't happen overnight but eventually his friend accepted the Lord.

Another friend made contact with a man whose spiritual background and understanding was nonexistent. He didn't know whether there was a God, didn't accept the Bible as authoritative, and certainly didn't think of Jesus Christ as the Savior. They met several times over a prolonged period, sometimes going out for breakfast and sometimes just talking. Eventually, the man came to believe that God existed, accepted the Bible as His Word to mankind, and trusted Jesus Christ as his Savior.

You probably have heard the term "24/7." That conveys the idea that something is going on twenty-four hours a day seven days a week. That should apply to your readiness to witness as well. Those in the early church who saw the resurrected Lord were "his witnesses unto the people" (Acts 13:31). The Lord told Paul that he would "be his witness unto all men of what thou hast seen and heard" (Acts 22:15). He went out from the Lord's appearance to him on the road to Emmaus "witnessing both to small and great" (Acts 26:22). Persecution forced many believers to flee to new parts of the Mediterranean region. "They that were scattered abroad went every where preaching the word" (Acts 8:4).

Life is short. Even for you who enjoy good health and live many years, it is brief in comparison to your eternal future. Job described his life as "swifter than a weaver's shuttle" (Job 7:6) and as "wind" (7:7) that rapidly passes away. His days passed "as the swift ships: as the eagle that hasteth to the prey" (9:26). Elsewhere, the Bible describes life as a flower that blooms briefly before it dies (James 1:10–11), as "short" (Ps. 89:47), and as "smoke" (Ps. 102:3) or a "vapour" (James 4:14) that rises into the sky and is gone. Since life is so short and uncertain, we need to use each day for God's glory. We do this best by obeying His Word in every area, including that of soulwinning.

Since you do not know how long you will live, there is only one way to be sure of using your life for the Lord. You must begin now and keep it up until your life ends. You may not have invested your time wisely in the past. You can't change that now, but you can make sure that you invest your future wisely. Start now to look for times when you can be a witness of God's saving grace.

By the way, there's no retirement from witnessing. One of the best soulwinners I have known was in his eighties. He would often walk up and down the main street of the town where he lived and engage people in conversation as they waited for the bus. He won many of them to the Lord. Another octogenarian friend had serious surgery. In the recovery period, a breathing tube was placed in his throat for several weeks. When the doctor finally removed the tube, his first words were "Doctor, do you know the Lord Jesus Christ as your Savior?"

The Bible tells us to use the present time. You don't need to learn the Bible from cover to cover before you start. Sam Jones, early twentieth-century evangelist, urged others, "Let's quit singing the 'Sweet By-and-by' and sing the 'Sweet-Now-and-now.'"[1] Romans 13:11 says, "It is [now] high time to awake out of sleep." A Christian should "no longer . . . live the rest of his time in the flesh to the lusts of men, but to the will of God" (I Pet. 4:2). "Now is the accepted time; behold, now is the day of salvation" (II Cor. 6:2). You should purpose to use your time today for witnessing to others as God gives you opportunities.

For most Christians, witnessing opportunities will come from those with whom you have close relationships, which may include your own family, relatives, neighbors, coworkers, members of a community group you are active in, school friends, and folks you have met casually but develop a special relationship with. The fact that you are close to these people gives you the opportunity to talk about spiritual things.

You can often develop close relationships with those whom you meet casually. When you are in a store, try to get to know the people who wait on you. Perhaps you can go to the same clerk each time and build a connection with him. How long has he worked there? Where did he grow up? Is he married? How many children does he have? In what part of town does he live? What does he think of current community issues? Over a period of time, your casual talk will lead to a friendly relationship and the opportunity to speak about the Lord.

You should take the same approach with others you may see more often. Shouldn't you work at establishing a closer link with some of your coworkers? Why not get to know your neighbors better? What about other parents whose children are involved in the same sports programs your children play in? Why not become friends with some of your extended family members?

Some of my friends hosted a block party to get to know their neighbors. A pastor invited his neighbor to go fishing. Another man volunteered to do yard or repair work for a widowed neighbor. A woman looked forward to visiting her neighbor over the fence, talking about everything as she built the relationship. A couple helped another couple move to a new home. Some friends helped a coworker move a piano. The list of examples is endless. There is no set pattern of activities for you to follow. The opportunities will vary from person to person. The key is to look for ways to turn your casual contacts into friendships.

You bring up a wide variety of topics when you are with close friends. I wouldn't start sharing my worries with another customer in line to pay at a store. I wouldn't start describing my collection of old woodworking tools to them. But I might very well share my concerns and interests with a close friend. Why not include spiritual topics in your conversations with these people?

A couple of my friends were involved professionally with another man. He happened to be of another religion. Over a couple of years, they would see each other at a monthly meeting. My friends gradually won his confidence and interest. They introduced him to a pastor who had come out of the same religious background as the man. By showing the biblical teaching about salvation, the pastor was able to lead him to accept Jesus Christ as his Savior.

Another friend took his car to the shop for some body work. He worked at getting to know the owner of the shop. Since he had some teenage sons who were driving, he had more than one opportunity to visit the shop. He invited the shop owner out for lunch, spoke with him about the Lord, and led him to receive the salvation that comes through the Lord alone.

Do you remember the Lord's last command? "But ye shall receive power, after that the Holy Ghost is come upon you: and ye shall be witnesses unto me both in Jerusalem, and in all Judaea, and in Samaria, and unto the uttermost part of the earth" (Acts 1:8). We start our witness in our "Jerusalem," the area in which we live. We then extend it to "Judaea, and in Samaria," the surrounding regions. As we have opportunity, we witness to "the uttermost part of the earth." This was the example of the believers in the book of Acts. In Jerusalem, "with great power gave the apostles witness of the resurrection of the Lord Jesus: and great grace was upon them all" (Acts 4:33). Later, they witnessed in the surrounding regions (Acts 8:25–40; 10:39). Finally, they went to the "uttermost part of the earth." To them, this included the world around the Mediterranean Sea. Later traditions tell us that the apostles carried the gospel to India, Parthia (modern-day Iran), Ethiopia, Media, and other nations a great distance from Palestine.

Your first witness should be to your Jerusalem, the area in which you live. The first group you should concern yourself with is your immediate family. Is your spouse a Christian? Do your children know the Lord as their Savior? You should work at maintaining a consistent testimony before those who know you best. Only by showing them your love for the Lord will they be persuaded to develop their own love for the Lord. Over my years in the ministry, I've worked with several thousand students. I've seen over and over that the best students tend to come from homes with godly parents. Homes in which the parents are lukewarm generally produce children who are lukewarm or even hostile toward Christianity.

You won't win your children to Christ in a session of a few minutes in which you explain the gospel to them. You may lead a child to profess faith in Christ simply because he wants to please you. But you'll win them more certainly with a life dedicated to the Lord. As they grow, they'll see what Jesus Christ has done for you. They'll see His guidance in the decisions you make. They'll see God's answers to your prayers. They'll see your devotion to Him. At some point, they'll be ready to ask the Lord to be their Savior. You may have the privilege of leading them to accept the Lord. That privilege, however, generally comes after several years of a godly testimony before them.

In addition to your immediate family, you may be close to other relatives. You may not see them often, but you feel the freedom to invite them over for dinner or to go to some social activity together. They're close enough to you that you think of them as friends. I have unsaved relatives I see only when I'm visiting in their area. I look forward to going out to eat with them or visiting in their home. It gives us a chance to catch up with each other. It also gives me the chance to talk with them about the Lord. I pray for them daily, and I'm looking forward to the time when they'll open their hearts to the Lord.

The New Testament teaches that Christians should show an evangelistic concern for friends. After the Lord had healed the maniac of Gadara, He "saith unto him, Go home to thy friends, and tell them how great things the Lord hath done for thee, and hath had compassion on thee" (Mark 5:19). In the parable of the lost sheep, the owner went into the wilderness, found the sheep, and carried it back. Then "he calleth together his friends and neighbours, saying unto them, Rejoice with me; for I have found my sheep which was lost" (Luke 15:6). The same thing happened in the parable of the lost coin. The woman searched her house until she found the coin. After she had found it, "she calleth her friends and her neighbours together, saying, Rejoice with me; for I have found the piece which I had lost" (Luke 15:9). These folks shared their good news with their friends. And that's what the Lord wants you to do with the gospel.

I once called on a woman whose name had come to the church. She told me how her nephew, who had recently accepted the Lord, had bubbled over with zeal in sharing his salvation with other members in the family. A group of us preached at jail and saw several men in a cell accept the Lord. For several months, until that group was transferred elsewhere, they did the evangelism. We would come week by week and find that they had already won other prisoners to the Lord. I visited a home in which a twelve-year-old girl had been taken by a neighbor to church. She had accepted the Lord. When I showed up at her home, I found that the young girl had already been telling her mother and two older sisters about Christianity. That's the kind of enthusiasm the Lord wants you to have, an enthusiasm that leads you to speak with your friends and neighbors about Christ.

It is common for friends and family members to show love for one another. This is a mark of Christians. The Lord taught, "Thou shalt love thy neighbour as thyself" (Mark 12:31). Paul wrote to the church at Rome that love for others summed up the entire Old Testament law (Rom. 13:9). The command to love neighbors as ourselves is the "royal law" (James 2:8). We should show our love "in deed and in truth" (I John 3:18). Further, we are commanded "that he who loveth God love his brother also" (I John 4:21).

What better way is there to show your love for someone else than by giving him or her the greatest gift a person can ever receive? Witnessing to your family and friends demonstrates your love. You want them to have eternal life. D. L. Moody put it this way: "The churches would soon be filled if outsiders could find that people in them loved them when they came. This draws sinners! We must win them to us first, then we can win them to Christ. We must get the people to love us, and then turn them over to Christ."[2] Anthony Groves, a nineteenth-century missionary to India, emphasized love with his comment, "Love and sacrifice are as inseparable as the sun and sunshine.

Sunshine is the sun sacrificing itself. Love is measured by sacrifice, by its gifts."[3] You show your love to your friends when you sacrifice your time and your resources so that others will have the opportunity to accept the Lord as their Savior.

CHAPTER TEN

FRUIT THAT REMAINS

YOUR RESPONSIBILITIES DO not end with leading someone to ask the Lord to save him. At that point the new convert is a spiritual baby. Just as a newly born child needs someone to care for him, so the newly born Christian needs someone to help him grow spiritually. He will remain a spiritual baby unless someone feeds him, exercises him, and guides him into growth. Since you have had the privilege of leading him to the Lord, you are the logical one to continue to work with him in spiritual areas.

You may recall Joe's decision to receive the Lord, back in chapter three. After his conversion, I gave him a Gospel of John to read. He had read it through by the next week. I then brought him a Bible and encouraged him to read in the New Testament. He began to read. Whenever he found something in his reading he didn't understand, he marked it in the margin and asked me about it the next week. For the following year, I had the privilege of guiding Joe in his study of God's Word, the Word that had brought him to salvation. After his release, he and his wife joined a local church, where they served the Lord through their activities.

Joe's story is typical of what you should do . . . as the Lord gives you the opportunity to follow up the initial decision. In many cases, it is awkward or impossible to provide help to the new Christian. The new convert may be a child or someone of the opposite sex. He may have a schedule that doesn't mesh with your schedule. The decision may come from someone when you are on an out-of-town trip.

Many of the men I have led to profess faith in Christ in jail were only there a week or two. After their court trial, they were transferred to other prisons where I had no access to them. The group of men that went to the jail to hold services on Sundays received permission from the jail to hold midweek services for the Christians. We went each Thursday night and preached directly to the Christians, trying to give what help we could in the short time we had with them. All too often, we had little opportunity to follow up after the decisions by the prisoners to receive the Lord. We did what we could.

Remember the driver in chapter six? Since I was only in his city one day, I could not continue to work with him. I did get his address and sent him a follow-up Bible study. I also recommended three fundamental churches in that city. Often, you'll have to do something similar to this. You can give the person some follow-up literature—a tract or a Bible study. You should guide him about getting into a church, Bible reading, and prayer. Often, you can find someone else who will be able to work with the person.

In many cases, you can invite new converts to your church. A sound, fundamental church with a teaching ministry is probably the best resource to help new converts grow. Some churches hold special classes for new believers. Most churches have Sunday school classes where you can fit into a group of similar ages and interests. Often, there is an evening time for Bible study before the church service. In many cases, the pastor will call on the new believers to acquaint them with the resources offered by the church.

You should still keep in contact with the new believers. Invite them out for coffee, have them over to the house for a meal, go with them to a ball game, or take them fishing and turn your conversations to spiritual things. Be alert for opportunities to encourage and teach them. In some cases, you can hold a simple Bible study with them in the middle of the week. You can personalize the study to meet their spiritual needs.

ASSURANCE OF SALVATION

There are some common topics every new Christian should study. One of the first things he needs is assurance of his salvation. The early church leader Augustine well said, "To be assured of our salvation is no arrogant stoutness. It is faith. It is devotion. It is not presumption. It is God's promise."[1]

Unfortunately, many people who have prayed to receive the Lord have no assurance that they are truly children of God. They look at a simple prayer when they asked the Lord to save them, they look at their life and don't see any great difference, and they go on not knowing whether they are on the road to heaven. That was the problem that Charles in chapter three had. You should address the topic. Personally, I try to take up assurance of salvation right after the decision has been made to receive the Lord. But you need to cover it later as well, reinforcing your initial teaching.

There are many verses in the New Testament that give assurance. "Verily, verily, I say unto you, He that heareth my word, and believeth on him that sent me, hath everlasting life, and shall not come into condemnation; but is passed from death unto life" (John 5:24). Notice the definiteness of the promise: "hath . . . shall not . . . is passed." The new convert should know what God has promised.

One of my favorite promises occurs in II Timothy 1:12. "For the which cause I also suffer these things: nevertheless I am not ashamed: for I know whom I have believed, and am persuaded that he is able to keep that which I have committed unto him against that day." That verse stands out to me since it is the verse that helped me settle my doubts about my own salvation.

The apostle John also taught that we can be assured of our salvation. "And this is the record, that God hath given to us eternal life, and this life is in his Son. He that hath the Son hath life; and he that hath not the Son of God hath not life" (I John 5:11–12). Eternal life comes through the Son of God. If you have the Son by faith, you have life. If you do not have the Son of God by faith, you do not have life. That's a clear statement. The new believer needs to understand that his salvation rests upon his relationship to the Lord. It does not rest on being baptized, joining a particular church or denomination, his ability to keep from sin, or anything else that he does or does not do. It rests only on his relationship to the Son of God.

The assurance of salvation should rest on a solid foundation. Knowing that he has received Christ as his Savior is part of that foundation. A second part of gaining assurance comes from an increased knowledge of God's Word. Paul touched on this when he wrote to Timothy, "Continue thou in the things which thou hast learned and hast been assured of [i.e., firmly persuaded of], knowing of whom thou hast learned them" (II Tim. 3:14). This is why it is so important to actively participate in a Bible-teaching church. In most churches, you have the opportunity for give-and-take in a Sunday school class or training hour where questions can be answered. You experience the traditional preaching of the Word of God as the pastor expounds the great truths of the Bible. There is the more casual interaction with believers that affords the opportunity to discuss matters of personal interest. All of these contribute to learning about the Bible. This learning helps you gain confidence regarding your relationship to the Lord.

The developing of a godly life with the fruit of good works is also an important element of gaining assurance. The apostle John touched on this in his first letter: "Hereby we know that we are of the truth, and shall assure [i.e., have confidence in] our hearts before him" (I John 3:19). This comment follows John's exhortation to the believers that they should practice charity to others in need (v. 17) and practice good works (v. 18). The author of Hebrews made this same emphasis: "For God is not unrighteous to forget your work and labour of love, which ye have shewed toward his name, in that ye have ministered to the saints, and do minister. And we desire that every one of you do shew the same diligence to the full assurance of hope unto the end" (Heb. 6:10–11). As the Christians carried on their "work and labour of love," they would gain assurance for the future hope of being with the Lord.

The start of the Christian life by placing faith in Christ, the study of God's Word that builds strength in the believer, and the service that Christians render to others—all these are necessary in gaining assurance of one's salvation. You can help the new believer take these steps as you work with him.

Assurance of Forgiveness for Sin

You should teach new Christians that Jesus Christ died for all their sins—past, present, and future. He didn't die for their past sins and then punish them for other sins that they commit after their salvation. He didn't die for their past sins and then expect them to do good works to atone for other sins. It is important that you show the new convert the extent of God's forgiveness for his sin. You might want to look at Micah 7:19: "He will turn again, he will have compassion upon us; he will subdue our iniquities; and thou wilt cast all their sins into the depths of the sea." Read Psalm 103:12 to them: "As far as the east is from the west, so far hath he removed our transgressions from us." Have the new Christian read Isaiah 38:17: "Behold, for peace I had great bitterness: but thou hast in love to my soul delivered it from the pit of corruption: for thou hast cast all my sins behind thy back." The sins of the Christian are in "the depths of the sea," removed from us "as far as the east is from the west," and placed "behind [God's] back." Taken together, that's a good description of sins that we will never face again.

The new believer may sin. In fact, he will sin. Christ died for that sin. It is already forgiven—as far as eternal punishment for sin is concerned. Sin, however, still has spiritual consequences. It causes a break in fellowship with the Lord. That shouldn't surprise anyone. If you offend a friend or neighbor or coworker, that offense brings about a break in the relationship. If you apologize, the relationship can be brought back into harmony again. The same is true with God. When you confess your sin to Him, He restores a harmonious relationship with you. The apostle John teaches this: "If we confess our sins, he is faithful and just to forgive us our sins, and to cleanse us from all unrighteousness" (I John 1:9). When the believer confesses his sin, God forgives and cleanses him.

Assurance of Victory over Sin

Many Christians fail at this point. They pray to receive the Lord as their Savior, and they are disappointed when they don't see immediate sinlessness in their lives. They don't understand that we live in sin-prone bodies in a sin-cursed world. In many cases, they have spent years in building strong habits of sin. Those habits won't always disappear overnight. When a baby learns to walk, he falls many times before he gains the strength and stability to talk without falling. Even then, he may find that he stumbles and falls after he has been walking for many years. Even as an adult I've fallen down. The same is true spiritually. The newly born Christian will fall into sin many times.

Brownlow North, a mid-nineteenth-century evangelist in Scotland and England, well said, "The whole question is not whether sin tempts or not, but whether it reigns or not."[2] The new believer needs to understand this. He may sin with a thoughtless word or action. As soon as he realizes what he has done, he should confess the sin to the Lord and make it right with the person he has offended. The sin brings a break in his fellowship with the Lord, but it does not cause him to lose the everlasting gift of salvation. He does not lose by his actions what he did not gain by his actions.

The new believer's victory over sin will generally come gradually, over a prolonged period of time. He learns to live the Christian life with practice. One by one, the old sins slip away and new habits of righteousness replace them. I grew up on Dixieland and Chicago jazz. My brother and I owned over five hundred records and albums, and we played them constantly in our room. But when I yielded myself to the Lord, that desire for worldly music slowly went away. The Lord replaced it with the enjoyment of Christian music. I remember the day at work when I was walking along, whistling "How Great Thou Art." I was not conscious of the change in my music until another engineer stopped me and introduced himself as a fellow Christian. The Lord had gradually changed me so that I delighted in music that honored Him.

Victory over sin is possible. Paul taught the Corinthians, "There hath no temptation taken you but such as is common to man: but God is faithful, who will not suffer you to be tempted above that ye are able; but will with the temptation also make a way to escape, that ye may be able to bear it" (I Cor. 10:13). In most cases, the victory over sin comes by simply turning and walking away from it. The young Christian needs to learn to leave activities and places where he will face temptation.

Peter echoes Paul's promise in II Peter 2:9: "The Lord knoweth how to deliver the godly out of temptations, and to reserve the unjust unto the day of judgment to be punished."

Jude speaks of "him that is able to keep you from falling" (Jude 24) into sin. Paul adds that "the Lord shall deliver me from every evil work" (II Tim. 4:18). The Lord has made provision for the young believer. As he grows spiritually stronger, he will see victory more and more often in his life.

IMPORTANCE OF BIBLE STUDY, PRAYER, AND FELLOWSHIP

God has given His will to the world in a single book, the Bible. Some churches may teach that they are the final standard for Christian living but that is not correct. God reveals His standards for life in the Bible and only in the Bible. New believers should begin to study the Bible in order to learn what God expects of them. They may study it at church, under the leadership of godly Sunday school teachers and pastors. They should also study it by themselves, spending time in reading and studying it every day. I've already stressed the part that the Bible plays in soulwinning in chapter three. I won't repeat that here except to say that you should teach new Christians to form a habit of spending time with God's Word.

Young believers should learn to pray. Many Christians don't spend much time in prayer. They may pray ritually before a meal, and they may pray from time to time about some special matter; but they often do not spend much time praying. Quite often, a person who is young in the faith doesn't know what to pray for or how to pray. You should teach them. You may want to study the teaching of the Lord in Matthew 6:9–13, as He taught the disciples to pray. You may simply discuss matters that ought to be prayed about—expressing love for the Lord, personal and family needs, testimony at work and with friends, the needs of the church, missionaries, special situations that come up from time to time, and so forth. Your guidance in this area will help the new convert rely on the Lord instead of on himself.

The Bible teaches the need for Christian fellowship: "I was glad when they said unto me, Let us go into the house of the Lord" (Ps. 122:1). "Not forsaking the assembling of ourselves together, as the manner of some is; but exhorting one another: and so much the more, as ye see the day approaching" (Heb. 10:25). In most cases, you will find your Christian friends from the people you meet at church. There are at least three purposes for being in church. Attending a good fundamental church helps you learn more about the Bible. It introduces you to Christian friends with whom you can enjoy friendship at other times away from church. It opens up opportunities for serving the Lord. Some Christians justify skipping church by saying something like, "I can worship God in nature" or "I can read the Bible on my own." That's true but there are other reasons for being in church. You can commune with nature at other times in the week. You can (and should) read the Bible at other times. But Christians should attend church regularly. New converts need to develop this practice.

IMPORTANCE OF OBEDIENCE

As the new believer grows spiritually, he will submit himself more and more to the Word of God. The new convert should understand that it is absolutely necessary that he follow the principles taught in the Bible. It is not enough to follow the practices of other Christians. We have churches filled with worldly Christians. If a new convert builds his Christian life on what he sees in other Christians, he will become worldly like them. If, however, he wants to please the Lord, Who has saved him, he will build his Christian life on God's Word.

There are good reasons that God sets certain standards in the Bible. The Bible teaches the need for wholesome speech: "Wherefore putting away lying, speak every man truth with his neighbour: for we are members one of another. . . . Let no corrupt communication proceed out of your mouth, but that which is good to the use of edifying, that it may minister grace unto the hearers" (Eph. 4:25, 29). What a believer says shows what he is. Profanity, lying, gossip, and other sins of speech reveal a wicked heart. Since a Christian has been cleansed from his sins, he should cultivate speech that honors the Lord. "I didn't mean anything by it" or "I was just kidding" or "Other Christians do it" are only excuses. The new believer needs to understand "that every idle word that men shall speak, they shall give account thereof in the day of judgment" (Matt. 12:36). They need to build habits of godly speech.

The Bible teaches that Christians should be honest. Paul wrote that the Christians at Rome should "provide things honest in the sight of all men" (Rom. 12:17). Peter urged his readers, "Having your conversation [or 'manner of life'] honest among the Gentiles: that, whereas they speak against you as evildoers, they may by your good works, which they shall behold, glorify God in the day of visitation" (I Pet. 2:12). It makes no difference what you have done in the past. From the time you receive the Lord as Savior, you should practice honesty.

A third area in which the young Christian should obey the Lord is that of witnessing. Young believers are often zealous. You should encourage them to tell others of their decision to accept the Lord and also to try to win others to the Lord. They don't have to know a lot about the Bible before they start. If they can mark a few verses in their Bibles and tell what the Lord has done for them, they're ready to witness. Too many Christians never tell anyone about the Lord. Try to start the new Christian on the right path.

As you follow up the new convert's decision to receive Christ as his Savior, you should tailor your studies to the needs of the person. Everyone's needs are different. Remember, your goal is "fruit that remains." As you are faithful in taking advantage of the opportunity to work with a young believer, you have tremendous potential for helping that person build a productive Christian life.

Is it worthwhile? Yes! I keep in my files a letter from a young man whom I led to the Lord. In it, he tells me that he is enrolling in a Christian college to prepare for the ministry. I look back to two young men I led to the Lord. Many years later, one of them was serving as a deacon in his church and the other was a leader in the high school group. I can think of a young woman who today serves the Lord in a Christian ministry. Others actively serve the Lord in local churches. These illustrate that the results of your soulwinning activities can become productive fruit that remains.

CHAPTER ELEVEN

THE RESOURCES SUMMARIZED

WE'VE TAKEN A leisurely look at many different resources. It may help you, however, to look at them all together. In reality, that's the way you'll use them. You will rarely rely on a single resource as you set out to win someone to the Lord. You may hand someone a tract with a Bible-based message and, at the same time, pray that the Holy Spirit will bring conviction to the person's heart. That's using five resources—the Bible, prayer, the Holy Spirit, a gospel tract, and your time. You may take time from your busy schedule to go through the Romans Road with a friend. That's giving up time as you use the plan of salvation in your witnessing. You may purchase some Bible-based stories to give to your Sunday school class. That's giving from your resources as you take advantage of an opportunity for service. You get the idea. Quite often, you blend several resources in your witnessing.

The Lord has given you many types of resources because different situations require you to use different approaches. And different approaches often require different resources. Some of the resources you've looked at are common to every witnessing situation. The work of the Holy Spirit is always needed. The message must always come from the Word of God. You will normally pray before, during, and after your witnessing.

Other resources may or may not be necessary. You won't always give out a tract when you witness. You won't always go step-by-step through the Romans Road in your witnessing. You won't always have the same opportunities available to you. You won't always find your soulwinning opportunities through a church ministry you're involved with. Since the circumstances in your witnessing will continually change, the Lord has given you different resources to draw on. In every situation, you have the resources you need.

Holy Spirit. The first and most important resource you have is God's Spirit working in the heart of the lost and guiding you as you present the gospel to some lost person. That's why you need to keep from sin and why you need to dedicate yourself completely to the Lord. You don't want to hinder the work of the Spirit through you in your witnessing.

Bible. Your witnessing must be based on the Word of God. Human reasoning and philosophy, logic, human-interest stories, and other man-made resources won't accurately convey the truth of the gospel. You must use the Bible in your witnessing. That's why you need to know what it says. Repeated over a number of years, your personal devotional time coupled with your Bible study, your memorization of verses, and your meditation on spiritual truths will give you a message that will point sinners to salvation.

Prayer. There is more power in prayer than most Christians ever see at work. When you witness, you should silently pray at the same time for God's guidance for you and for His conviction in the other person. You should keep yourself free from sin and regularly pray as you rely on the Lord in your life. In that way, it will be natural for you to bring the Lord into your witnessing through prayer.

Tracts. You should make it a habit to carry good gospel tracts with you. Since you don't always know in advance when an opportunity to witness will arise, you should always be ready. Having an attractive, well-written gospel tract can help you reach others. It may lead to a conversation, or it may do its own preaching after you've left. The experience that many have had in using tracts argues strongly that they are helpful in winning the lost.

Practical Matters. I've mentioned several practical matters that you should practice. You should witness to everyone you can talk with about Christ, not take salvation for granted, be willing to put yourself out, take advantages of ministry opportunities in your local church and other opportunities that present themselves, and be persistent. You have the ability—if you don't feel confident now, a little training and a little experience will give you the confidence you need.

Giving. Giving is part of being obedient to the Word of God. Your willingness to give makes it possible for both you and your church to carry on soulwinning activities. While you may not be personally involved in bringing forth the fruits of your giving, you have an important part in every soul that comes to Christ through your local church . . . if you have been faithful in giving. You may not see the fruits of your giving to missions, but the missionary cannot carry on his ministry without people like you who support missions. As you give of your time, your resources, and your money, you further the cause of evangelism.

Plan of Salvation. You should have a plan to your witnessing. You should memorize your approach. This will give you confidence as you approach someone about the Lord. While questions may arise that cause you to digress, having a plan will let you come back to it and continue your witness to a lost person.

Time. In virtually every witnessing opportunity, you will spend time that could have been invested in something else.

The use of your time requires you to set priorities. Since the value of a soul involves eternity, nothing else should have a higher priority. You should always be ready to sacrifice a few minutes as you tell the good news of salvation to others.

This short summary is enough to show you that you have every resource you need. You may think of something else you can draw on that is unique to your situation. But whether you do or not, you have all the resources you need. What you need now is action! You should actively set out to witness to others. Is your family saved? If not, that's a good place to start. What about your neighbors? Your coworkers? Your friends at the golf course? Are you sure that the couple you sit next to at church are saved? Do you have a hobby that you share with friends? Are you involved in some youth organization—Boy or Girl Scouts, Little League, Pop Warner football? A political group? Be tactful. Be wise. But be on the lookout for lost souls who need someone to speak with them about the Lord.

ENDNOTES

INTRODUCTION

[1] The Barna poll on a variety of religious subjects is located at www.barna.org on the Internet.

[2] Carl Sandburg, *Abraham Lincoln: The Prairie Years*, vol. 1, quoted by Shirley Streshinsky, *Audubon* (New York: Random House, 1993), p. 60.

[3] Quoted from *Confessions* 9.8, by Michael Marshall, *The Restless Heart: The Life and Influence of St. Augustine* (Grand Rapids, MI: William B. Eerdmans, 1987), p. 19.

[4] L. C. Rudolph, *Francis Asbury* (Nashville: Abingdon Press, 1966), p. 154.

[5] Andrew Woolsey, *Duncan Campbell—a Biography: The Sound of Battle* (London: Hodder and Stoughton, 1974), p. 35.

[6] Wilbur M. Smith, *A Watchman on the Wall: The Life Story of Will H. Houghton* (Grand Rapids, MI: Wm. B. Eerdmans, 1981), p. 42.

[7] Quoted by Jonathan Goforth, *Rosalind Goforth* (Minneapolis, MN: Bethany House, 1974), p. 147.

CHAPTER ONE

[1] Charles L. Allen, *What I Have Lived By* (Old Tappan, NJ: Fleming H. Revell, 1976), p. 24.

[2] Dennis J. Hester, *The Vance Havner Quotebook* (Grand Rapids, MI: Baker Book House, 1986), p. 83.

[3] Percy O. Ruoff, *The Spiritual Legacy of George Goodman* (London: Pickering and Inglis, 1949), p. 108.

[4] Salu Daka Ndebele with Dan Wooding, *Guerilla for Christ* (Old Tappan, NJ: Fleming H. Revell, 1979), p. 107.

CHAPTER TWO

[1] Two of the three words, καρπός and γέννημα (and their derivatives), may occur with a metaphorical sense, referring to spiritual fruit. The third word, ὀπώρα, occurs only once, in Rev. 18:14, where it refers to literal fruit that is eaten.

[2] Quoted by Rosalind Goforth, *Jonathan Goforth* (Minneapolis, MN: Bethany House, 1986), p. 135.

CHAPTER THREE

[1] Martin Luther, *Luther's Works*, ed. and trans. Theodore G. Tappert, LIV (Philadelphia: Fortress Press, 1967), p. 165.

[2] L. C. Rudolph, *Francis Asbury* (Nashville: Abingdon Press, 1966), p. 141.

[3] Roger J. Green, *Catherine Booth* (Grand Rapids, MI: Baker Books, 1996), p. 24.

[4] Basil Miller, *George Muller: Man of Faith and Miracles* (Minneapolis: Bethany House, 1941), p. 22.

[5] Miller, p. 138.

[6] Adapted from www.forerunner.com/forerunner/X0205_John_Quincy_Adams.html

[7] Laura McElwaine Jones, *The Life and Sayings of Sam P. Jones* (Atlanta: Franklin-Turner, 1907), p. 463.

[8] Bernard Ruffin, *Fanny Crosby: The Hymn Writer* (Uhrichsville, OH: Barbour, 1995), pp. 24, 29.

[9] John Bunyan, *Grace Abounding to the Chief of Sinners* (Grand Rapids, MI: 1948), pp. 22–23.

[10] Elisabeth Elliot, *Shadow of the Almighty: The Life and Testament of Jim Elliot* (New York: Harper and Brothers, 1958), p. 11.

[11] Quoted by Rosalind Goforth, *Jonathan Goforth* (Minneapolis: Bethany House, 1986), p. 29.

[12] J. Murray Murdoch, *Portrait of Obedience: The Biography of Robert T. Ketcham* (Schaumburg, IL: Regular Baptist Press, 1979), p. 30.

[13] G. H. Lang, *Anthony Norris Groves: Saint and Pioneer* (London: Thynne and Co. 1939), p. 57.

[14] Richard Ellsworth Day, *Rhapsody in Black: The Life Story of John Jasper* (Philadelphia: Judson Press, 1953), p. 107.

Chapter Four

[1] L. C. Rudolph, *Francis Asbury* (Nashville: Abingdon Press, 1966), p. 141.

[2] Hunter B. Blakely, *Religion in Shoes: Brother Bryan of Birmingham* (Richmond: John Knox Press, 1953), p. 88.

[3] Basil Miller, *Mary Slessor: Heroine of Calabar* (Minneapolis: Bethany House, 1974), p. 138.

Chapter Five

[1] Laurie Walthers, *Sowing and Reaping* (Greenville, SC: Gospel Fellowship Association, January-March, 1990), p. 2.

[2] Oren Vallejo, missionary prayer letter, June, 1993.

[3] Personal letter from Paul Levin to Jon Bright, May 25, 1995.

[4] Aubry Walter Mutch, *A Study of Christian Tracts and Methods for Their Distribution* (Dissertation, Bob Jones University, June, 1949), p. 76.

[5] George Verwer, *Literature Evangelism* (Bromley, Kent, England: STL Books, 1977 rpt. 1980), p. 9.

[6] Verwer, p. 11.

[7] Verwer, p. 15.

[8] Paul Levin, *Share Christ Through Tract Evangelism* (Normal, IL: Bible Tracts, n.d.), p. 1.

[9] E. Henry Edwards and Faris D. Whitesell, *Sowing Gospel Seed: The Tract User's Handbook* (Chicago: Moody Press, 1954), p. 10.

[10] Edwards and Whitesell, p. 124.

Chapter Six

[1] Ron Hamilton, "Obedience." (Greenville, SC: Majesty Music, 1981).

[2] Daniel A. Del Rio, *Simón Bolívar* (Clinton, MA: Bolivarian Society of the United States, 1965), p. 9.

Chapter Seven

[1] Faith Cook, *William Grimshaw of Haworth* (Edinburgh: Banner of Truth Trust, 1997), p. 210.

[2] Percy O. Ruoff, *The Spiritual Legacy of George Goodman* (London: Pickering and Inglis, 1949), p. 127.

[3] William Elliot Griffis, *A Maker of the New Orient* (New York: Fleming H. Revell, 1902), p. 94.

[4] D. Shelby Corlett, *Spirit-Filled: The Life of the Rev. James Blaine Chapman* (Kansas City, MO: Beacon Hill Press, n.d.), p. 192.

[5] Internet: www.barna.org, May 19, 2003.

[6] Adapted from George Hawker, *The Life of George Grenfell: Congo Missionary and Explorer* (New York: Fleming H. Revell, 1909), p. 22.

[7] Lettie B. Cowman, *Charles E. Cowman: Missionary-Warrior* (Los Angeles: Oriental Missionary Society, 1928), p. 81.

Chapter Nine

[1] Laura McElwaine Jones, *The Life and Sayings of Sam P. Jones*, p. 457.

[2] Richard Ellsworth Day, *Bush Aglow* (Philadelphia: Judson Press, 1936), p. 146.

[3] G. H. Lang, *Anthony Norris Groves: Saint and Pioneer* (London: Thynne and Co. 1939), p. 69.

Chapter Ten

[1] J. A. Wood, *Perfect Love* (published by the author, 1881), p. 131.

[2] Kenneth Moody-Stuart, *Brownlow North: The Story of His Life and Work* (London: Hodder and Stoughton, 1879), p. 77.